AMERICA'S NATIONAL PARKS

GLACIER
NATIONAL PARK

ADVENTURE, EXPLORE, DISCOVER

DAVID ARETHA

MyReportLinks.com Books
an imprint of

Enslow Publishers, Inc.
Box 398, 40 Industrial Road
Berkeley Heights, NJ 07922
USA

MyReportLinks.com Books, an imprint of Enslow Publishers, Inc. MyReportLinks®
is a registered trademark of Enslow Publishers, Inc.

Copyright © 2009 by Enslow Publishers, Inc.

Library of Congress Cataloging-in-Publication Data

Aretha, David.
  Glacier National Park : adventure, explore, discover / David Aretha.
     p. cm. — (America's national parks)
  Includes bibliographical references and index.
  ISBN-13: 978-1-59845-088-0 (hardcover)
  ISBN-10: 1-59845-088-3 (hardcover)
  1. Glacier National Park (Mont.)—Juvenile literature. I. Title.
  F737.G5A74 2008
  978.6'52—dc22

                       2007017396

Printed in the United States of America

10 9 8 7 6 5 4 3 2 1

To Our Readers:
Through the purchase of this book, you and your library gain access to the Report Links that specifically
back up this book.
The Publisher will provide access to the Report Links that back up this book and will keep these Report
Links up to date on **www.myreportlinks.com** for five years from the book's first publication date.
We have done our best to make sure all Internet addresses in this book were active and appropriate when
we went to press. However, the author and the Publisher have no control over, and assume no liability
for, the material available on those Internet sites or on other Web sites they may link to.
The usage of the MyReportLinks.com Books Web site is subject to the terms and conditions stated on the
Usage Policy Statement on **www.myreportlinks.com**.
A password may be required to access the Report Links that back up this book. The password is found
on the bottom of page 4 of this book.
Any comments or suggestions can be sent by e-mail to comments@myreportlinks.com or to the address
on the back cover.

♻ Enslow Publishers, Inc., is committed to printing our books on recycled paper. The paper in every
book contains 10% to 30% post-consumer waste (PCW). The cover board on the outside of each book
contains 100% PCW. Our goal is to do our part to help young people and the environment too!

Photo Credits: APN Media, LLC, p. 14; Civilian Conservation Corps Legacy, p. 48; C.O.C.E.E.C., p. 75;
© Corel Corporation, pp. 3, 52, 63, 85, 97; Defenders of Wildlife, p. 69; Holt-Atherton Special
Collections, p. 116; howstuffworks.com, p. 106; istockphoto.com, pp. 6 (goat, St. Mary Lake); 6–7 (top);
7 (waterfall); 8–9, 12–13, 33, 38–39, 60–61, 98–99, 102–103; lewis-clark.org, p. 67; Library of
Congress, pp. 25, 28; LiveScience, p. 89; MyReportLinks.com Books, p. 4; NASA, p. 58; National Park
Service, pp. 5, 42, 94, 113; National Park Service/Glacier Natural History Association, p. 40; National
Park Service/Melissa Wilson, p. 111; NPCA, p. 109; NSIDC, p. 19; PBS, p. 27; Photos.com, pp. 6 (hik-
ers); 76, 92–93; Project Gutenberg Literary Archive Foundation, p. 30; Shutterstock.com, pp. 7 (bighorn,
bear); 16–17, 22–23, 46, 56–57, 64–65, 70, 82–83; Sierra Club, p. 36; State of Montana, p. 11;
SwissEduc, p. 87; terragalleria.com, p. 96; *The Chicago Tribune*, p. 90; The *Missoulian*, pp. 35, 44;
University of Montana, p. 81; USAtoday.com, p. 24; USDA, p. 114; U.S. Fish and Wildlife Service, p. 72;
USGS, pp. 47, 78.

Cover Photo: Photos.com (background); Shutterstock.com (mountain goat).

CONTENTS

MyReportLinks.com Books
Great Books, Great Links, Great for Research!

The Internet sites featured in this book can save you hours of research time. These Internet sites—we call them **"Report Links"**—are constantly changing, but we keep them up to date on our Web site.

When you see this "Approved Web Site" logo, you will know that we are directing you to a great Internet site that will help you with your research.

Give it a try! Type http://www.myreportlinks.com into your browser, click on the series title and enter the password, then click on the book title, and scroll down to the Report Links listed for this book.

The Report Links will bring you to great source documents, photographs, and illustrations. MyReportLinks.com Books save you time, feature Report Links that are kept up to date, and make report writing easier than ever! A complete listing of the Report Links can be found on pages 118–119 at the back of the book.

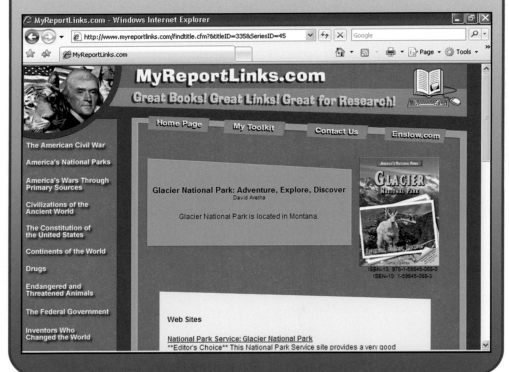

Please see "To Our Readers" on the copyright page for important information about this book, the MyReportLinks.com Web site, and the Report Links that back up this book.

Please enter GNP1560 if asked for a password.

WATERTON
LAKES
NATIONAL
PARK

Middle
Waterton
Lake

Blood
Indian
Reserve

Cameron
Lake

Lower
Waterton
Lake

BRITISH COLUMBIA
MONTANA

CANADA
UNITED STATES

ALBERTA
MONTANA

Kintla
Lake

Mount Cleveland
10,466 ft.
3,190 m.

GLACIER

Bowman
Lake

Quartz
Lake

Lower
Quartz Lake

Many Glacier
Information

Lake
Sherburne

Saint Mary
Visitor Center

Polebridge

NATIONAL

Grace
Lake

The Loop

Weeping
Wall

Logging
Lake

PARK

Mt. Oberlin
8,180 ft.
2,493 m.

Logan Pass
Visitor Center

Going-to-the-Sun Road

Saint Mary Lake

Blackfeet

Indian

Reservation

Trail of the Cedars Nature Trail
McDonald
Falls

Hidden
Lake

Jackson Glacier Overlook

Avalanche
Lake

Reynolds Mtn.
9,125 ft.
2,781 m.

Red
Eagle
Lake

Huckleberry Mtn.
6,593 ft.
2,009 m.

Lake McDonald

Going-to-the-Sun Road

Medicine
Grizzly
Lake

North Fork Cut
Bank Creek

Apgar Visitor Center

Triple Divide Peak
8,020 ft.
2,444 m.

Two
Medicine
Lake

Lower Two
Medicine
Lake

FLATHEAD

NATIONAL

FOREST

Lake
Isabel

LEWIS & CLARK

NATIONAL

Continental Divide

FOREST

Walton

FLATHEAD

NATIONAL

FOREST

North
0   5   10 Kilometers
0   5   10 Miles

This map shows some of the popular spots in and around Glacier National Park.

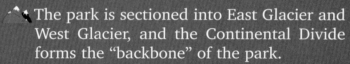

- Glacier National Park was established on May 11, 1910.

- The park is located in northwest Montana and shares a border with Alberta, Canada.

- Glacier National Park encompasses 1,584 square miles (4,101 square kilometers).

- The park is sectioned into East Glacier and West Glacier, and the Continental Divide forms the "backbone" of the park.

- The Flathead National Forest rests along Glacier's western and southern borders.

- The Blackfeet Indian Reservation lies next to Glacier's eastern border.

- The park's terrain includes mountains, valleys, glaciers, lakes, forests, and prairies.

- Mount Cleveland is Glacier's tallest mountain at 10,466 feet (3,192 meters).

- Lake McDonald and St. Mary Lake are the park's largest bodies of water.

- Hundreds of species of animals and more than one thousand species of plants are found within its borders.

- Mountain goats, bighorn sheep, grizzly and black bears, moose, elk, bald eagles, and bull trout are among Glacier's noteworthy animals.

- Glacier National Park includes about 30 glaciers and more than 130 named lakes.

PARK FACTS

- Scientists predict that the park's remaining glaciers will melt by 2030.

- Going-to-the-Sun Road, which bisects the park and crosses the Continental Divide, is a National Historic Civil Engineering Landmark.

- Favorite activities include sightseeing, hiking, camping, fishing, biking, and boating.

- The Waterton-Glacier International Peace Park was established in 1932.

- Glacier National Park and Waterton Lakes National Park were designated by the United Nations as Biosphere Reserves in 1976 and World Heritage sites in 1995.

- The park is open year-round, although many roads are closed from fall to spring.

- Glacier National Park attracts close to 2 million visitors per year.

- Seven-day admission is $25 per vehicle.

- Glacier Park International Airport is located in nearby Kalispell, Montana.

- The park's operating budget for the fiscal year 2006 was $11,885,000.

- Telephone: (406) 888-7800.

- Mailing address: Glacier National Park, PO Box 128, West Glacier, Mont. 59936.

Chapter

1

A spectacular view of the mountains from Going-to-the-Sun Road.

Driving to Paradise

t happens every spring. The snow in the land of glaciers finally melts, and Going-to-the-Sun Road opens to the public. From all over America, thousands flock to Glacier National Park to experience a drive through paradise.

If Montana is indeed the "Treasure State," then Glacier is home to its natural jewels. At Glacier, declared *National Geographic*, the "mountains seem sharper, the air purer, other animals more numerous and easier to spot. Glacier jolts you alive like no other place."[1]

Glacier National Park, which hugs the Canadian border, encompasses 1.4 million acres of "Big Sky Country." The northern mountains of the Continental Divide bisect the park, but these mountains are unlike any other. Millions of years ago, enormous glaciers chiseled and carved this land into a natural masterpiece. "There are mountains, and then there are mountains," wrote a recent visitor to the park. "While all of them have their own beauty and character and should be seen, those in Glacier are simply awe-inspiring."[2]

Going-to-the-Sun Road transports you to this magical place. As you ascend higher and higher, indulge in the mountainous beauty. And if you are afraid of heights, don't look down! Travel writer Susan Bayer Ward wrote that Going-to-the-Sun Road "will set your heart (and, in one stretch, your nerves) on fire."[3]

The road stretches fifty-two miles (83.7 kilometers) from east to west and actually crosses the Continental Divide. If you start your journey in the early evening and head east, the sun will illuminate the scene in front of you. Soon you will reach McDonald Falls, where water roars down large rocks into flumes below. When you reach Trail of the Cedars, get out of the car. Stroll along the trail's boardwalk and explore a dense forest of cedar and hemlock.

As you drive on, the road takes you higher into the mountains. A ten-mile (16.1-kilometer) stretch features massive rock called the Garden Wall. Small waterfalls tumble down its sides, and wildflowers adorn its valleys. Bird Woman Falls

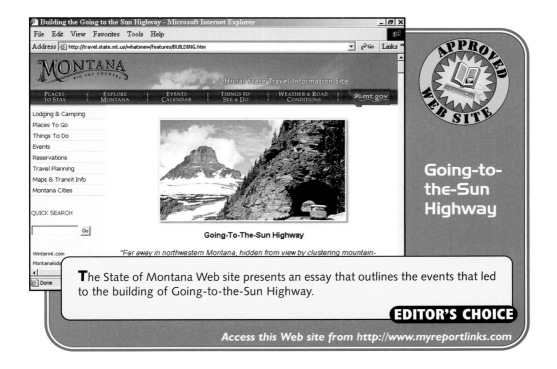

Going-To-The-Sun Highway

"Far away in northwestern Montana, hidden from view by clustering mountain-

The State of Montana Web site presents an essay that outlines the events that led to the building of Going-to-the-Sun Highway.

EDITOR'S CHOICE

Access this Web site from http://www.myreportlinks.com

Overlook and the Weeping Wall highlight this fantastic stretch of roadway. Eventually you reach the road's pinnacle at Logan Pass. You are more than 6,600 feet (2,011 meters) above sea level, in the heart of the Continental Divide.

Get out of your vehicle and witness the spectacle around you. Barefaced mountains plunge into lush, green valleys. Lakes, streams, waterfalls, and flowers enhance the spectacle. Look above for a mountain goat or a bighorn sheep perched on a high cliff. Perhaps you will catch your first glimpse of a black bear or even a grizzly bear.

Continuing east, you'll begin your descent. At Jackson Glacier Overlook, witness one of the

A mountain goat perched on a ledge amidst Glacier National Park's mountains.

Glacier National Park (part of Waterton-Glacier International Peace Park) | Oh, Ranger! - Microsoft Internet Ex...

File   Edit   View   Favorites   Tools   Help

Address   http://www.ohranger.com/glacier

Oh, Ranger!

For Answers To
All Your Questions™

In Depth

○ Glacier National Park (part
  of Waterton-Glacier
  International Peace Park)
○ Activities & Programs
○ American Indians Today
○ At Your Fingertips
○ Be
○
○
○ H
○ Histo

Glacier National Park

Glacier National Park (part of Waterton-Glacier International Peace Park)

Glacier National Park encompasses a region of mountains in the northwest corner of Montana that abuts Waterton Lakes National Park in southwestern Alberta. Glacier's pristine forests, alpine meadows, rugged mountains, spectacular lakes, and 700 miles of trails, Glacier is a hiker's paradise. Discover what awaits you and relive the days of old through historic chalets, lodges, transportation, and stories of Native Americans.

Glacier National Park at a Glance provides an online tour of the park. Information about Glacier's bear population, ecology, and history is included. Visitor information and an article on the preservation of the park round out the content.

park's trademark glaciers. Sun Point offers a spectacular view of St. Mary Lake—encased, it seems, by a circle of mountains. Finally, the road flattens out as you reach the eastern prairies. Two Dog Flats is a native grassland community where deer, elk, and little mammals like to roam.

Glacier National Park, founded in 1910, is part of a much larger ecosystem. An ecosystem is a community of animals, plants, microorganisms, and the environment in which they interrelate. Glacier's ecosystem also includes Canada's Waterton

Lakes National Park, which is immediately north of Glacier National Park. In fact, the two parks form the Waterton-Glacier International Peace Park. The Flathead National Forest, which surrounds half of Glacier's borders, is also part of the ecosystem.

Each year, Glacier's attendance approaches 2 million, making it one of the most visited national parks in the United States. Its large attendance is remarkable considering its remote location and cold climate. Glacier's unique terrain and natural beauty are the charms that lure the tourists.

One avid cyclist, who has visited more than seventy countries, wrote that Glacier National Park "is really unique terrain. The mountains are just gorgeous; I don't think you can find shapes like this." The cyclist added that "my body, my brain, and my spirit just feel better at 6,600 feet."[4]

American citizens have delighted in Glacier since the 1800s. Moreover, American Indians have respected—even worshipped—this land for hundreds of years. Today, however, the park faces serious threats and challenges, most notably the melting of its trademark glaciers.

Let's venture back in time to learn the complete story of Glacier National Park. We will need to start at the very beginning, more than one billion years ago.

Chapter 2

A view of Chief Mountain in the northeast area of Glacier. The Blackfeet Indians considered this mountain and others in the park to be sacred and mystical.

A Billion Years of History

When visitors stand amid the mountains of Glacier National Park, they begin to understand why the Blackfeet Indians respected this land so much. Humans have inhabited the territory for a few thousand years, but that is only a blink in time for these mighty mountains. The mountains have been fixtures of the landscape for many millions of years, and their origin can be traced back 1.5 billion years.

At that time, geologists believe, a shallow sea covered the area. Highlands bordered the sea on the east, north, and south. Rivers, streams, and rain carried sediment down the sea's coast and along the seabed. Not much would accumulate in a day, but over hundreds of millions of years the sediments transformed into rock—approximately four miles thick.

The bottom parts of these rock layers make up the mountains that stand today. On some of these formations, we can see the ripple marks, fossilized algae, and mud cracks that were formed. But here's the most amazing fact about these mountains: hundreds of millions of years ago, they lay forty miles west of their present location.

→ MOVING MOUNTAINS

Close to 200 million years ago, an earthshaking event began on the western edge of the North American continent. Massive slabs of earth, called crustal plates, collided underneath the continent. It was not a sudden crash, but a slow, powerful push that occurred over millions of years. Old, hard rock moved up and over younger, softer rock. At the points of collision, the continent bulged upward.

The results were chains of mountains throughout the West, most notably the Rocky Mountains. About 70 million years ago, the Rockies began to rise. The slab on which Glacier National Park and Waterton Lakes National Park currently rest moved an amazing distance—forty miles (64.4 kilometers) to the east. The cliffs that we see on the east side of Glacier were the eastern edge of that migrating slab.

Eventually, tens of millions of years ago, the crustal collisions ended. After that, erosion began to shape the mountains. The upper layers were worn down and rounded. Over millions of years, river water cut valleys into the mountains. Little plants called lichens grew on the rock, and their acids created cracks. Water entered the cracks and, when it froze, expanded the crevices. After sand and plant matter settled in the cracks, trees and bushes began to grow in them. Yet, since this is Glacier National Park, cold weather must have developed. Sure enough, about 3 million years ago, a great ice age began.

ALL ICE

During this sustained period of frigid weather, snow filled up the valleys and nearly piled up to the mountaintops. The mile-high snow was so compact that most of it turned to ice.

These huge masses of ice were too heavy to remain on the sides of mountains. Gradually, they

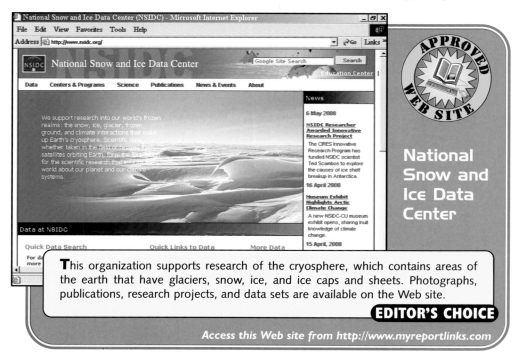

National Snow and Ice Data Center

This organization supports research of the cryosphere, which contains areas of the earth that have glaciers, snow, ice, and ice caps and sheets. Photographs, publications, research projects, and data sets are available on the Web site.

EDITOR'S CHOICE

Access this Web site from http://www.myreportlinks.com

moved downward, thus becoming glaciers, which are slowly moving masses of ice. As the glaciers moved down the mountains, they picked up boulders and rocks. With their great weight and jagged bottoms, the massive ice hunks carved U-shaped valleys. The park's upper McDonald Creek Valley is a spectacular example of this formation.

⮕GLACIERS SCULPT THE LAND

The glacial period of the last ice age did not end until about eleven thousand years ago. Up to that time, glaciers carved and shaped the land of the Glacier area. As the glaciers moved down the mountainsides, they pushed earth to the sides as well as forward. The glaciers acted like a conveyor belt, carrying rocks and other debris from the side walls of the mountains.

The rock that piled up on the sides is called a lateral moraine. Some of these moraines became mountain ridges, such as Snyder Ridge on the western side of the park. The earth pushed forward by the glaciers is called a terminal moraine. Some of the pushed earth formed dams. Lake McDonald and the valley surrounding it were carved when an estimated 2,200-foot-thick (670-meter) glacier melted and could not escape a terminal moraine.[1]

Like magnificent tools, the glaciers sculpted the land in many fascinating ways. When several glaciers carved different sides of a mountain, they formed a horn. Mount Reynolds at Logan Pass exemplifies the horn shape. Some glaciers gouged bowl-shaped depressions, called cirques, into the ground. The water that fills these is called a tarn. Iceberg Lake and Avalanche Lake are examples of this.

Arêtes were formed when two glaciers gouged the earth next to each other, forming a long and narrow ridge. Glacier's Garden Wall, which separates Lake McDonald Valley from Many Glacier Valley, is the park's most famous arête. Some smaller glaciers carved little valleys—called hanging valleys—high on the mountainsides. Water fills these valleys and then pours out of their mouths, creating spectacular waterfalls. Bird Woman Falls on Mount Oberlin cascades out of a hanging valley.

⇒ GLACIERS GOING AWAY

The giant glaciers melted more than ten thousand years ago, but smaller glaciers formed several thousand years ago. These glaciers were tiny compared to those from the earlier ice ages, but they still chiseled away at the mountains. By 1850, an estimated one hundred and fifty glaciers remained in the area. After that, due to global warming, most of them melted away. Today, only about

Avalanche Lake, a mountain pool carved out by glaciers.

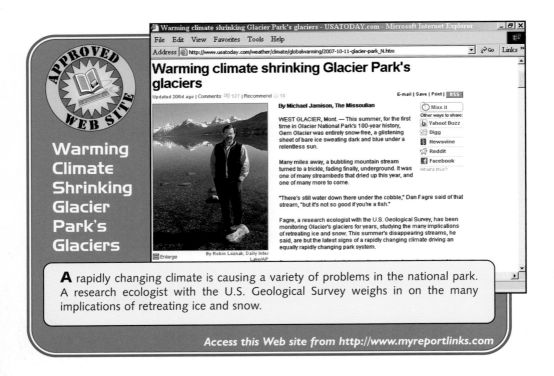

Warming Climate Shrinking Glacier Park's Glaciers

A rapidly changing climate is causing a variety of problems in the national park. A research ecologist with the U.S. Geological Survey weighs in on the many implications of retreating ice and snow.

Access this Web site from http://www.myreportlinks.com

twenty-seven glaciers remain—and they are getting smaller every year.

⟳ BLACKFEET RULE

Humans have occupied the Glacier region for thousands of years. By the mid-1700s, the Blackfeet emerged as the dominant tribe. Two theories explain how this tribe got its name. One suggests that black was the color of their moccasins' soles. Another theory states that they once walked over a burned prairie and were dubbed "Blackfeet" by another tribe.

The warlike Blackfeet were protective of the eastern prairies of Montana and Alberta. On these lands roamed enormous herds of bison, which Blackfeet and rival tribes prized as a food source. American Indians referred to these bison-laden prairies as hunting grounds. The Kalispel, Flathead, and Kootenai tribes made incursions from the west. They traversed the gaps of Glacier's mountains to reach the hunting grounds. But the Blackfeet would not allow such trespassing. They crossed the mountains themselves and raided their enemies' camps.

▲ *This group of Blackfeet Indians is singing in front of a tepee.*

Despite their ferocity, the Blackfeet were deeply spiritual. These American Indians, and those of other tribes, considered the mountains of Glacier and Waterton to be mystical and sacred. They especially revered Chief Mountain, located in the northeast area of Glacier. This isolated rock, they believed, symbolized the powerful medicine of these mountains.

WHITE TRAPPERS AND TRADERS

In the late eighteenth century, white men of European descent made their first appearance in the Glacier area. The many bison and the stories of spirits in the mountains did not concern them. They came to hunt beaver, which were plentiful in the mountain streams. Easterners and Europeans coveted beaver fur, making beaver trapping in the West a lucrative business.

David Thompson, a British trapper, likely was the first white man to write about the northern Rockies. "At length the Rocky Mountains came in sight like shining white clouds in the horizon," he wrote of the Canadian Rockies in 1787, "and as we proceeded they rose in height, their immense masses of snow appeared above the clouds and formed an impassible barrier, even to the eagle."[2]

In the late 1700s, white traders and trappers began to barter with the Blackfeet. As the years passed, more and more white people appeared.

In 1806, the Lewis and Clark expedition explored the Marias River, thus coming within fifty miles (80.5 kilometers) of what is now Glacier National Park. Their well-publicized journey stirred interest in the Rockies among fur traders.

In 1810, Scottish trader Finian MacDonald and two others were the first-known white men to enter present-day Glacier. They did not stay for long, as Blackfeet warriors chased them away at Marias Pass. Other traders realized that they shouldn't mess with the Blackfeet. Not until mid-century did white men return to the area.

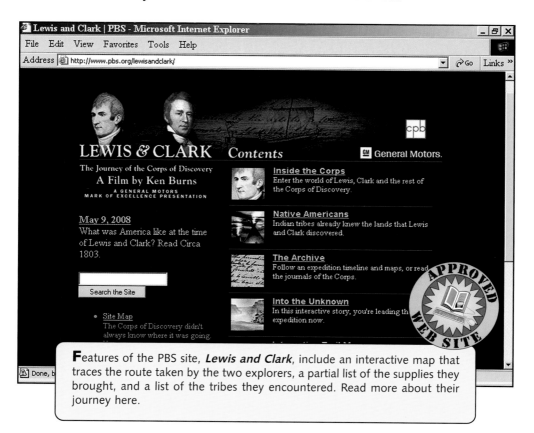

Features of the PBS site, *Lewis and Clark*, include an interactive map that traces the route taken by the two explorers, a partial list of the supplies they brought, and a list of the tribes they encountered. Read more about their journey here.

⊖DEMISE OF THE BLACKFEET

By the 1850s, the fur trade business had largely died out. Whites, however, arrived in the Glacier area with higher purposes. Government surveyors came to mark the boundary between the United States and Canada. Missionaries arrived to convert American Indians to Christianity. In addition, railroad scouts came to find a pass through the Rocky Mountains.

In the mid- and late 1800s, the U.S. government was determined to build transcontinental railroads. Great locomotives would carry people and goods to the West quickly, thus populating the vast western regions. Of course, the Rocky Mountains were a tremendous roadblock for railroad companies. It was extremely difficult, if not impossible, to establish railroad tracks in high mountain terrain. For years, explorers searched around Glacier, trying to find a clear, low pass through the mountains. In the 1850s, Washington Territory governor Isaac Stevens pressured northwestern American Indian tribes into signing treaties. These tribes gave up land that whites used to develop railroads.

Railroads were the bane of American Indians' existence. Their construction led to the establishment of railroad towns and an increase in white settlers. In such scenarios across the West, whites would hunt bison, killing off the tribes' main food source. Moreover, wars over land often erupted between whites and the American Indians.

Most frightening of all, white men and women transmitted diseases, such as smallpox, to the American Indians. While the whites had inherited immunity to these diseases, the Indians had none. Thus, large numbers of American Indians died from these diseases. A smallpox epidemic in 1837 killed an estimated six thousand Blackfeet.

Marias Pass, the Blackfeet knew, was the best path for a railroad through the Glacier region. In fact, Marias was the lowest mountain pass through all of the Rocky Mountains. However, the Blackfeet kept the whereabouts of Marias Pass a secret. They deliberately deceived railroad scouts,

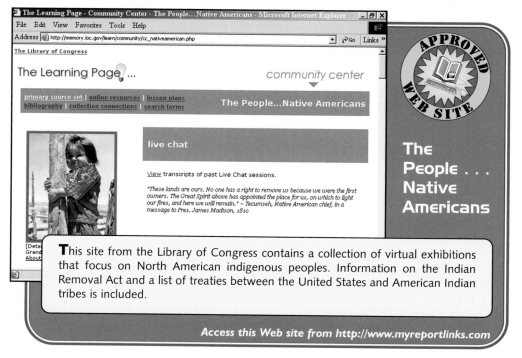

The Learning Page - Community Center - The People...Native Americans - Microsoft Internet Explorer

File   Edit   View   Favorites   Tools   Help

Address   http://memory.loc.gov/learn/community/cc_nativeamerican.php   Go   Links »

The Library of Congress

The Learning Page...   community center

primary source set | online resources | lesson plans
bibliography | collection connections | search terms   The People...Native Americans

live chat

View transcripts of past Live Chat sessions.

"These lands are ours. No one has a right to remove us because we were the first owners. The Great Spirit above has appointed the place for us, on which to light our fires, and here we will remain." ~ Tecumseh, Native American chief, in a message to Pres. James Madison, 1810

APPROVED WEB SITE

The People . . . Native Americans

This site from the Library of Congress contains a collection of virtual exhibitions that focus on North American indigenous peoples. Information on the Indian Removal Act and a list of treaties between the United States and American Indian tribes is included.

Access this Web site from http://www.myreportlinks.com

telling them that other routes were the best places to look.

It wasn't until 1889 that a white man discovered Marias Pass. John F. Stevens, an explorer for the Great Northern Railway, unraveled the mystery. Within two years, a railroad line was constructed through the Glacier area. Work camps arose nearby, two of which developed into towns: Belton and Midvale.

By that time, the Blackfeet could not mount any resistance. The tribe was confined to the Blackfeet Reservation, and smallpox ran rampant. And when the last of the bison were killed in the area, Blackfeet began to starve. Many of these American Indians died of hunger during the

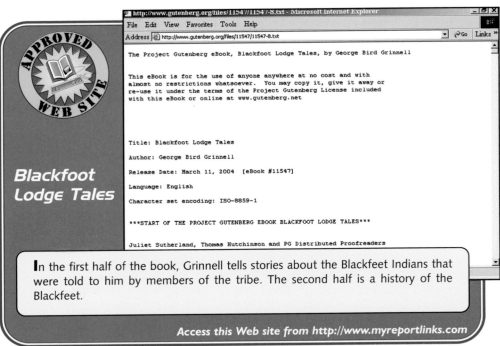

APPROVED WEB SITE

Blackfoot Lodge Tales

> http://www.gutenberg.org/files/11547/11547-8.txt - Microsoft Internet Explorer
>
> File   Edit   View   Favorites   Tools   Help
>
> Address http://www.gutenberg.org/files/11547/11547-8.txt   Go   Links »
>
> The Project Gutenberg eBook, Blackfoot Lodge Tales, by George Bird Grinnell
>
> This eBook is for the use of anyone anywhere at no cost and with
> almost no restrictions whatsoever. You may copy it, give it away or
> re-use it under the terms of the Project Gutenberg License included
> with this eBook or online at www.gutenberg.net
>
> Title: Blackfoot Lodge Tales
>
> Author: George Bird Grinnell
>
> Release Date: March 11, 2004 [eBook #11547]
>
> Language: English
>
> Character set encoding: ISO-8859-1
>
> ***START OF THE PROJECT GUTENBERG EBOOK BLACKFOOT LODGE TALES***
>
> Juliet Sutherland, Thomas Hutchinson and PG Distributed Proofreaders

In the first half of the book, Grinnell tells stories about the Blackfeet Indians that were told to him by members of the tribe. The second half is a history of the Blackfeet.

Access this Web site from http://www.myreportlinks.com

winters of 1883 and 1884. Seemingly few whites cared about their plight, with James Willard Schultz a notable exception.

⇒ SCHULTZ INSPIRES GRINNELL

In the 1870s, Schultz traveled to the West because he wanted to shoot bison. He became fascinated with the Blackfeet, joining the tribe and marrying a Blackfeet woman. He even participated with American Indian friends in raids against other tribes.

Schultz would go on to write extensively about the Blackfeet and the nearby mountain region. In 1885, one of his articles caught the attention of George Bird Grinnell, the editor of *Forest and Stream* magazine. Reading Schultz's article "To the Chief Mountain," Grinnell became enchanted by the imagery: mountain goats and bighorn sheep, sparkling blue lakes walled in by towering peaks. Schultz had even written about a glacier.

The article inspired Grinnell to check out this northern paradise. That fall, he, Schultz, and a Blackfeet named Yellow Fish hunted in the region's mountains. In the midst of a blizzard, Grinnell killed a bighorn sheep on Singleshot Mountain. In Swiftcurrent Valley, the men attempted to climb an enormous glacier that one day would be named after Grinnell. The Blackfeet even made the editor a member of their tribe.

In fifteen weekly articles for *Forest and Stream*, Grinnell described his extraordinary trip to northern Montana. In one piece, he wrote:

> Here, serrated ridges and horn-shaped peaks reign over a jumble of turquoise lakes, waterfalls, cascades, river valleys, hanging gardens, and alpine meadows. Born of geologic and glacial violence, this random landscape couldn't be more perfect had it been designed and executed by Michelangelo. Like the ocean, its sheer scope has a way of putting humanity in its place.[3]

Grinnell's articles popularized the region, and he continued to promote the area long afterward. In 1887, he returned and drew a map of the region. He named mountain peaks after friends and business associates. Later, the U.S. Geological Survey would borrow his map and keep most of the names.

LOBBYING IN WASHINGTON

Grinnell's opinions carried a lot of political weight. He helped influence the U.S. Congress to provide regulations for national parks. He founded the Audubon Society to save the birds of North America. And he informed President Theodore Roosevelt about the slaughter of big-game animals in the West. Grinnell also was the driving force in making Glacier a national park.

Grinnell first noted this thought in his diary in 1891. It would take many years before the park

The Weeping Wall, a waterfall that pours down onto Going-to-the-Sun Road.

came to be, but Grinnell continued to be heavily involved in the region. In 1895, he was among those involved in negotiating the purchase of land from the Blackfeet. The tribe's chief, White Calf, authorized the sale of the area. They sold about eight hundred thousand acres to the United States for $1.5 million.

The government acquired all of the tribe's land east of the Continental Divide up to a certain boundary. The Blackfeet would live on a reservation east of that boundary. During negotiations and in subsequent years, Grinnell urged fair treatment of the tribe. He and Schultz also honored American Indians by naming features of the park after Indian legends.

CAMPAIGNING FOR A PARK

Congress officially designated the Glacier area as a "Forest Preserve" in 1900, but it remained open to mining and homesteading.[4] In the early 1900s, miners invaded the land. They prospected for gold, copper, and oil, but their efforts proved unsuccessful.

In the first decade of the century, Grinnell and others lobbied for making the territory a national park. With such status, the area would be entitled to better governmental protection. As of 1900, only four national parks existed in the United

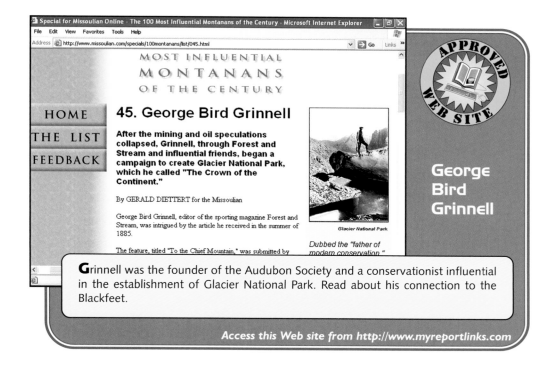

Special for Missoulian Online - The 100 Most Influential Montanans of the Century - Microsoft Internet Explorer

File   Edit   View   Favorites   Tools   Help

Address   http://www.missoulian.com/specials/100montanans/list/045.html   Go   Links »

MOST INFLUENTIAL
MONTANANS
OF THE CENTURY

HOME

THE LIST

FEEDBACK

45. George Bird Grinnell

After the mining and oil speculations collapsed, Grinnell, through Forest and Stream and influential friends, began a campaign to create Glacier National Park, which he called "The Crown of the Continent."

By GERALD DIETTERT for the Missoulian

George Bird Grinnell, editor of the sporting magazine Forest and Stream, was intrigued by the article he received in the summer of 1885.

The feature, titled "To the Chief Mountain," was submitted by

Glacier National Park

Dubbed the "father of modern conservation."

George Bird Grinnell

Grinnell was the founder of the Audubon Society and a conservationist influential in the establishment of Glacier National Park. Read about his connection to the Blackfeet.

Access this Web site from http://www.myreportlinks.com

States: Yellowstone, Sequoia, Yosemite, and Mount Rainier.

In a 1901 article in *Century* magazine, Grinnell called the mountainous region in northern Montana the "Crown of the Continent." The Great Northern Railway joined the campaign, too. The railway officials believed that a national park would increase tourist train travel to that area.

John Muir, the legendary nature lover, also praised this glorious land. As he eloquently wrote in 1901:

Get off the track at Belton Station, and in a few moments you will find yourself in the midst of what you are sure to say is the best care-killing country on the continent—beautiful lakes derived straight from glaciers, lofty mountains steeped in lovely . . . blue skies and clad with forests and glaciers, mossy, ferny waterfalls in their hollows, nameless and numberless, and meadowy gardens abounding in the best of everything.[5]

Certainly, the momentum was building to name the area a national park. Three other national parks were declared in the early 1900s. They included Crater Lake in 1902, Wind Cave in 1903, and Mesa Verde in 1906. Many believed that the region in northern Montana should be next.

⊜ GRINNELL'S DREAM COMES TRUE

In December 1907, Senator Thomas Carter—with Grinnell's support—introduced a bill to create

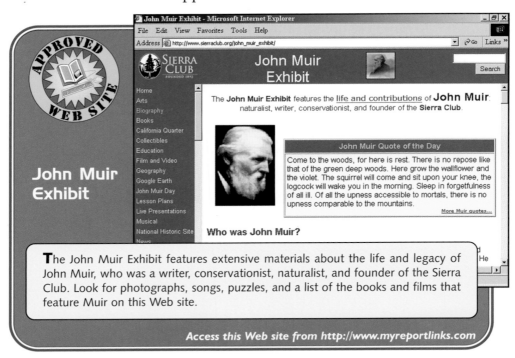

John Muir Exhibit

The John Muir Exhibit features extensive materials about the life and legacy of John Muir, who was a writer, conservationist, naturalist, and founder of the Sierra Club. Look for photographs, songs, puzzles, and a list of the books and films that feature Muir on this Web site.

Access this Web site from http://www.myreportlinks.com

the park. The bill was strongly opposed by the residents of Kalispell, a nearby town. Carter introduced another bill in February 1908. That bill passed the Senate but died in the House of Representatives.

Carter's third bill finally passed, and President William Howard Taft signed it into law on May 11, 1910. The legislation called for the creation of Glacier National Park, preserving sixteen hundred square miles (4,144 square kilometers) of wilderness. While Senator Carter introduced the bills, Grinnell deserved much of the credit. He replied, humbly: "To receive credit for good work well done is pleasant, but a reward far higher . . . comes from the consciousness of having served the public well."[6]

In 1925, Grinnell was awarded the Theodore Roosevelt Distinguished Service Medal. President Calvin Coolidge told him: "Few have done as much as you . . . to preserve vast areas of picturesque wilderness for the eyes of posterity. . . . The Glacier National Park is particularly your monument."[7] For nearly a century, Grinnell has been hailed as the "Father of Glacier National Park."

Chapter

3

Sunrise over glaciers and a lake at Glacier National Park.

Glacier's First Century

The act that established Glacier National Park called for preserving the park in a state of nature. Yet the park was also meant to be like Yellowstone National Park, which was created as a "pleasuring ground for the benefit and enjoyment of the people."[1] These two goals contradicted each other. How could Glacier be preserved while at the same time be developed into a hot tourist destination? It could not. The developers—with the money and power—won out.

As soon as the act was signed in May 1910, the Great Northern Railway (GNR) began construction efforts. James J. Hill, the GNR's "Empire Builder," hoped to develop Glacier into the "Playground of the Northwest." Thousands of tourists each year, he envisioned, would pay for train tickets to the magnificent new park. During the summer of 1910, construction crews built a chalet complex at Belton. The GNR planned to build more chalets—plus hotels, tent camps, roads, and trails—on Glacier's east side.

In later decades, national park officials would become preoccupied with preserving nature. But that wasn't so much the case in the 1910s and 1920s. Stephen Mather, the National Park Service director from 1917 to 1929, stated: "Scenery is a hollow enjoyment if the tourist starts out after an indigestible breakfast and a fitful sleep on an impossible bed."[2]

Glacier's first superintendent, William R. Logan, encouraged the park's development. He said early in his reign, "It is the desire of my heart

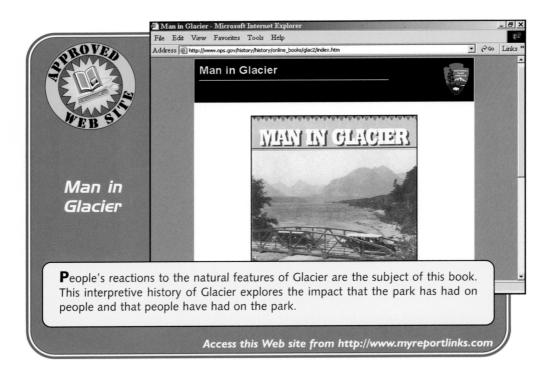

Man in Glacier

Man in Glacier - Microsoft Internet Explorer

File   Edit   View   Favorites   Tools   Help

Address http://www.nps.gov/history/history/online_books/glac2/index.htm

Man in Glacier

People's reactions to the natural features of Glacier are the subject of this book. This interpretive history of Glacier explores the impact that the park has had on people and that people have had on the park.

Access this Web site from http://www.myreportlinks.com

to make this park the most wonderful land in the world."[3] Before making progress, however, Logan faced a natural disaster. In the summer of 1910, more than one hundred thousand acres of forest fires raged in all areas of the park. From the distance on the Blackfeet Reservation, the tribespeople watched the land that they held sacred burn day after day.

⇒ CONSTRUCTION BOOM

After the fires, business continued to boom at Glacier National Park. Mining activity was allowed in the park, as was the harvesting of dead or diseased timber. The U.S. Department of the Interior urged the cutting of trees to allow hotel construction. Others sought to build telephone lines and administrative buildings.

Louis Hill, James J. Hill's son, supervised construction efforts at Glacier. He purchased land from the Blackfeet Indian Reservation and used it for the construction of the Glacier Park Lodge. The hotel, which cost $500,000 to build, opened in 1913. Within the park, more chalets, trails, and tepee camps were built.

The Great National Railway advertised the park using the marketing phrase "See America First," to encourage wealthy Americans to visit Glacier National Park rather than the Alps. The tourists came in droves. Vacationers took the

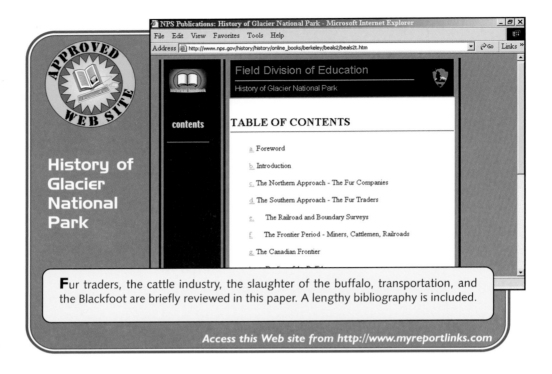

NPS Publications: History of Glacier National Park - Microsoft Internet Explorer

File   Edit   View   Favorites   Tools   Help

Address http://www.nps.gov/history/history/online_books/berkeley/beals2/beals2t.htm   Go   Links »

Field Division of Education

History of Glacier National Park

History of Glacier National Park

contents

TABLE OF CONTENTS

Fur traders, the cattle industry, the slaughter of the buffalo, transportation, and the Blackfoot are briefly reviewed in this paper. A lengthy bibliography is included.

Access this Web site from http://www.myreportlinks.com

Great Northern Railway to the outskirts of the park. They stayed at the lodge or the log-and-stone chalets, and they rode horseback through the park. In 1915, the GNR completed the Mammoth Mountain Hotel, which became known as the "showplace of the Rockies." The hotel resembled a Swiss chalet and had many stunning features. Included was a painting stretching 180 feet long that was painted by a dozen Blackfeet.

By 1915, Glacier had become an extremely popular destination. In fact, its twenty-eight thousand visitors that year exceeded the total of visitors to Yellowstone National Park. Though car touring was popular in Yellowstone, Glacier visitors stuck with horses. In 1925, the Saddle Horse Company supplied horses for about ten thousand Glacier tourists.

Nevertheless, road construction continued in Glacier National Park throughout the 1920s. Roads were built on both the east and west sides of the park. However, no road existed to connect the two sides, as the mountains of the Continental Divide stood as a seemingly impassible obstacle. But beginning in the mid-1920s, several companies took on the challenge.

GOING TO THE SUN

Once completed, the new road would traverse Glacier's east prairies, go up and over Logan Pass, and cut through forest on the west side of the park. At first, it was called the Transmountain Highway. Eventually, it would be renamed Going-to-the-Sun Road.

From 1925 to 1929, three hundred men worked on this one roadway. The most difficult work was blasting and clearing thousands of tons of rock. Much of it had to be cleared by hand because machines could not operate on the steep terrain. On the east side, workers faced the daunting task of constructing a four-hundred-foot-long (122-meter-long) tunnel. To get down to the job site, workers had to climb a hundred-foot (30.5-meter) rope from the edge of a cliff. One laborer

Restoring the Road

Engineering marvel

FROM THE START, SUN ROAD WAS DESIGNED TO BE SPECTACULAR

WEST GLACIER - Tom Osborn leans out the driver's side window of his Jeep Cherokee, watching the wheels as he inches the big blue rig into a narrow mountain pullout.

A hand-width beyond his right front tire, the fractured roadside empties into a thousand feet of vertical nothing, thin air dropping onto the green carpet of treetops below. A few inches beyond his bumper - glowing orange with a Florida license plate - a single stone, maybe half a foot high, serves as guardrail against the plunge.

Written by
MICHAEL JAMISON

Jammer bus drivers Aubrey Chapman, front, and Bill Lindsay bring the first tour group over Logan Pass on July 15, 1933.
T.J. HILEMAN/Glacier National Park Archives

A marvel of engineering, Going-to-the-Sun Road was built across the alpine heights of Glacier National Park. At this site, **From the Start, Sun Road Was Designed to Be Spectacular**, learn more about the men who helped to build the road.

lost his grip on the rope and plunged sixty feet (18.3 meters) to his death—the only fatality on the project.

On July 15, 1933, a grand celebration marked the opening of the $3 million Going-to-the-Sun Road. The new roadway—with its majestic mountain views—had an enormous effect on tourism. As Glacier historian C. W. Buchholtz wrote: "Going-to-the-Sun Road became an overnight success at drawing motorists, and it developed into a major attraction of Glacier National Park. Some estimates indicate that over 95 percent of all park visitors centered their entire visit along the roadway. . . ."[4]

U.S. Highway 2, just south of Glacier, opened in 1930. Park attendance increased to seventy-four thousand in 1930. Attendance then nearly tripled—to 210,000—in 1936. In addition to heavy traffic that year, park officials sweated through the Heavens Peak Fire. The flames destroyed many Park Service buildings, and they nearly engulfed the Many Glacier Hotel. This followed the Halfmoon Fire of 1929, which ravaged fifty thousand acres of forest.

➲ PEACE AT THE BORDER

In 1932, history was made at the boundary of Montana and Alberta, Canada. The mountains of Glacier National Park did not stop at the Canadian border, but extended north of the border. Back in 1895, Canada named its portion of this wilderness Waterton Lakes National Park. In 1932, Rotary International members worked to create the Waterton-Glacier International Peace Park. The combined park was meant to symbolize the bonds of friendship and peace between the citizens of the two countries.

Canadian vacationers were allowed to cross the border to enjoy Glacier National Park. Of course, the opposite was also true. Many Americans

Going-to-the-Sun Road, which was completed in 1933. The stunning views seen from the road have made it a favorite attraction for visitors.

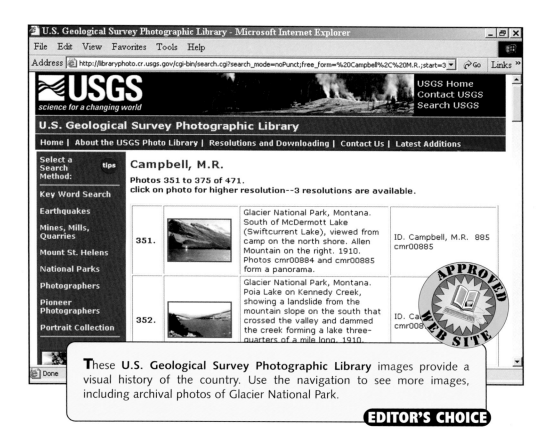

U.S. Geological Survey Photographic Library - Microsoft Internet Explorer

File   Edit   View   Favorites   Tools   Help

Address http://libraryphoto.cr.usgs.gov/cgi-bin/search.cgi?search_mode=noPunct;free_form=%20Campbell%2C%20M.R.;start=3   Go   Links »

USGS
science for a changing world

USGS Home
Contact USGS
Search USGS

U.S. Geological Survey Photographic Library

Home | About the USGS Photo Library | Resolutions and Downloading | Contact Us | Latest Additions

Select a
Search   tips
Method:

Key Word Search

Earthquakes

Mines, Mills,
Quarries

Mount St. Helens

National Parks

Photographers

Pioneer
Photographers

Portrait Collection

Campbell, M.R.

Photos 351 to 375 of 471.
click on photo for higher resolution--3 resolutions are available.

| 351. | | Glacier National Park, Montana. South of McDermott Lake (Swiftcurrent Lake), viewed from camp on the north shore. Allen Mountain on the right. 1910. Photos cmr00884 and cmr00885 form a panorama. | ID. Campbell, M.R. 885 cmr00885 |
| 352. | | Glacier National Park, Montana. Poia Lake on Kennedy Creek, showing a landslide from the mountain slope on the south that crossed the valley and dammed the creek forming a lake three-quarters of a mile long. 1910. | ID. Ca cmr008 |

APPROVED WEB SITE

These **U.S. Geological Survey Photographic Library** images provide a visual history of the country. Use the navigation to see more images, including archival photos of Glacier National Park.

EDITOR'S CHOICE

Done

booked rooms at the Canadian park's Prince of Wales Hotel.

All tourists realized that Glacier was a place of fun and danger. Park workers entertained vacationers with supervised hikes and tours, floral displays in hotels, and songfests in the evenings. Yet in the park's early years, people died by falling off cliffs or into crevices. Others were killed by drowning, falling rock, or exposure to the elements. Glacier was indeed a playground, but a seriously hazardous one.

→DEPRESSION AND WAR

During the 1930s, the Great Depression hurt business throughout the United States. Ironically, the troubled times actually benefited Glacier National Park. On March 31, 1933, the federal government established the Civilian Conservation Corps (CCC). The government paid unemployed young men to work on conservation-minded projects, such as planting trees and maintaining parks. That very year, 1,600 CCC workers arrived to improve conditions at Glacier National Park.

These laborers began cleaning up the burned area caused by the 1929 fire. They cut old snags and sawed them into logs and lumber. By 1936,

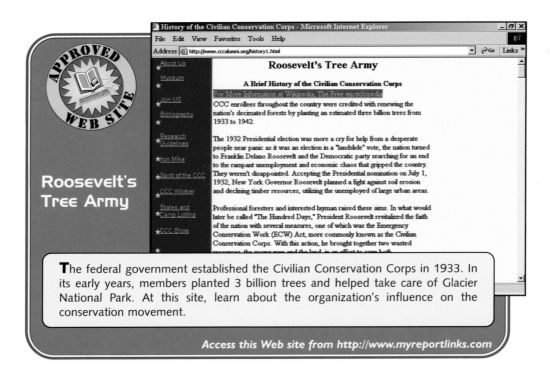

The federal government established the Civilian Conservation Corps in 1933. In its early years, members planted 3 billion trees and helped take care of Glacier National Park. At this site, learn about the organization's influence on the conservation movement.

Access this Web site from http://www.myreportlinks.com

more than two hundred railroad cars shipped lumber out of the park. Glacier's CCC workers engaged in numerous other projects, including roadside cleanup and the construction of trails and campgrounds. When the CCC finally left in the early 1940s, Glacier National Park was better than ever. As journalist Ernie Pyle enthusiastically said, "I wouldn't trade one square mile of Glacier for all the other parks put together."[5]

Glacier boasted an attendance of 180,000 in 1941. But that was before the United States became fully embroiled in World War II. In 1943, attendance fell to just twenty-three thousand. Many of the park's rangers joined the armed forces, and Glacier's staff was greatly reduced. Some conscientious objectors—those who refused to enlist in the military due to religious or moral reasons—were assigned to work at the park. During these lean years, many unused and dilapidated chalets were torn down.

THE DAM CONTROVERSY

By war's end, Americans were eager to enjoy life. Tourism at Glacier skyrocketed, surpassing three hundred thousand in 1947. Park officials struggled to handle the great increase of tourists. They needed more hotels and campgrounds, more stores and picnic areas. In the late 1940s, the park service faced another scare: the Army Corps of

Engineers pushed for the creation of the Glacier View Dam. The dam would provide both electricity and flood control for the region. However, about twenty thousand acres (8,094 hectares) of the park would be lost.

Park Service Superintendent J. W. Emmert denounced the proposed plan. So did many citizens, conservation groups, and politicians. U.S. Senator Burton Wheeler of Montana said: "To seriously curtail one of the few great recreational areas at a time when expansion, rather than decrease is needed, seems tragic."[6] The Army Corps of Engineers eventually backed off, and the plan was scrapped.

A MONEYMAKER

In the 1950s, it was tourists—not water—that flooded Glacier National Park. In 1951, five hundred thousand visitors poured through the park gates. These vacationers pumped more than $12 million into the local economy. While the Blackfeet endured difficult economic conditions on their reservation, Glacier had become big business.

Local business owners wanted each year's tourist season to start as early in the spring as possible. This meant that heavy, melting snow had to be cleared off the roads. This was a dangerous undertaking, since both workers and snow could easily tumble down the mountains. In May 1953, two workers died during such a situation. One of the men, Bill Whitford, fell three hundred feet (91.4 meters) to his death. Road crews continued to face this peril every spring. The needs of tourists, and the money they spent, were considered more important than workers' safety.

⮕MISSION 66

By 1954, the American economy was booming. Millions of people packed up their Fords and Chevys and headed west for summer vacations. Six hundred thousand people visited the park in 1954. Expecting even greater numbers in the future, park officials launched the largest construction program in Glacier's history. They called this $23 million project "Mission 66," since the completion date was set for 1966.

Most of the program involved renovation and reconstruction. Laborers repaired existing roads, trails, bridges, and buildings, and officials also added new features to the park. Workers expanded campgrounds, added picnic tables and "comfort stations," and built housing for Park Service employees.

Glacier officials also devoted more resources to the ecology of the park. Scientists began to make animal census reports and study Glacier's wildlife more carefully. They found, for example, that elk herds were overpopulating Glacier's east side. To correct the problem, elk were harassed to the point where they left the area.

→ RAIN, FIRE, AND TRAGEDY

In the mid-1960s, three alarming events vaulted Glacier into the national spotlight. In early June 1964, sudden warm weather and rain caused a massive rush of snow and water to pour down the mountain streams. Lakes overflowed and valleys flooded. Trails, roads, bridges, and hotels were

▲ The land alongside McDonald Creek was carved by glacial flooding.

deluged and damaged. Officials considered some trails and bridges too ruined to repair.

In 1967, dry conditions and an electrical storm led to a series of fires beginning on August 11. More than three thousand firefighters worked into September to control the blazes. While these fires raged, tragedy struck on August 13. Two grizzly bears mauled and killed two nineteen-year-old women, Michele Koons and Julie Helgeson. Grizzlies had always been considered dangerous, but these were the first recorded deaths by grizzly bears in the park's history.

The deaths caused a public outcry about animal management in Glacier. The Park Service determined that too much garbage—specifically, discarded food—littered the park, attracting bears to campsites. After this horrific incident, officials strictly enforced proper garbage disposal. In addition, rangers better informed visitors about park safety.

Eco-Conscious

In the late 1960s and 1970s, an environmental movement swept the nation. Americans became concerned about preserving nature, not exploiting it. Glacier weathered its share of controversy. Many were appalled to hear that sewage from the Logan Pass Visitor Center had flowed into Reynolds Creek and St. Mary Lake. Other nature lovers criticized Park Service superintendent William J. Briggle for claiming that he wanted to develop Glacier even more. As Jim Rice of Whitefish, Montana, stated: "I'd like to remind Superintendent Briggle that he is bound by law to protect Glacier and all that is enclosed by its boundaries. I for one frankly hope he devotes the bulk of his time to that goal, rather than promotion."[7]

Glacier's management responded positively. It created programs to improve pollution problems and study the park's ecological issues. In 1976, the United Nations honored Glacier by selecting it as a World Biosphere Reserve. Such reserves were created "to promote and demonstrate a balanced relationship between humans and the biosphere."[8]

Thus, by the 1970s, few shared James J. Hill's original dream of making Glacier the "Playground of the Northwest." Instead, citizens seemed to adopt the beliefs of the Blackfeet: the beautiful wilderness of Glacier should be enjoyed but, most of all, respected.

⊖ BATTLING BLAZES

In 1995, Glacier was named a World Heritage Site, signifying its international importance. Unfortunately, the park's history over the last two decades has been marked by frightening fires. While the great fire in Yellowstone National Park stole headlines in 1988, Glacier National Park lost twenty-seven thousand (10,926 hectares) acres to flames that year. Firefighters also battled exceptional blazes in 1994, but the big one came in 2003. Beginning in mid-July, fires burned a full 10 percent of Glacier National Park. One fire threatened the historic Granite Park Chalet, and it advanced across Going-to-the-Sun Road.

Fires, however, are a natural part of Glacier's ecosystem. In subsequent seasons, new vegetation emerges in the once-charred landscape, and eventually animals return to these areas. In recent decades, glacier officials have developed a fire management plan. While they try to prevent and suppress human-caused fires, they monitor most natural fires. Firefighters try to douse natural fires only if they become too big and/or pose a threat to humans and structures.

While the 2003 fires crippled tourism to Glacier that summer, vacationers returned in big numbers in subsequent years. The park is currently undergoing major renovation projects. Campgrounds, visitor centers, historic hotels, and Going-to-the-Sun Road are all getting an upgrade. Officials want their park to shine in time for the big celebration planned for 2010. That year will mark the one-hundredth anniversary of Glacier National Park.

Chapter

4

The mountain goat is one of the more interesting creatures roaming Glacier National Park.

Full of Life

George Grinnell found just the right words when he dubbed Glacier National Park the "Crown of the Continent." Its sharply defined peaks and valleys resemble the shape of a crown. The region stands tall—both in latitude and altitude. And it is majestic and regal, like a king or a queen.

More than anything else, mountains dominate Glacier National Park and the surrounding area. The great Continental Divide splits the park, which includes not one but two mountain ranges: the Lewis Range and the Livingston Range. Seven mountains soar above 10,000 feet (3,048 meters), with Mount Cleveland the tallest at 10,466 feet (3,190 meters).

Glacier National Park is surrounded by protected land. While the park itself consists of 1,584 square miles, the protected region that surrounds it is ten times that size. To the north, Canada's Flathead Provincial Forest and two massive Canadian

parks, Waterton Lakes National Park and the
Akamina-Kishinena Provincial Park, border Glacier. The Blackfeet Indian Reservation lies to the
east, and the Flathead National Forest swaddles
Glacier in the west and south.

WATER, WATER EVERYWHERE

When the snow atop Glacier's Triple Divide Peak
area melts, it flows down many streams and
rivers. These lead in to three completely different
directions. Some of the waterways pour into the
Columbia River, which leads to the Pacific Ocean.
Others flow into the Missouri River, which leads to
the Mississippi River and eventually the Gulf of
Mexico. Finally, some of Glacier's stream and river

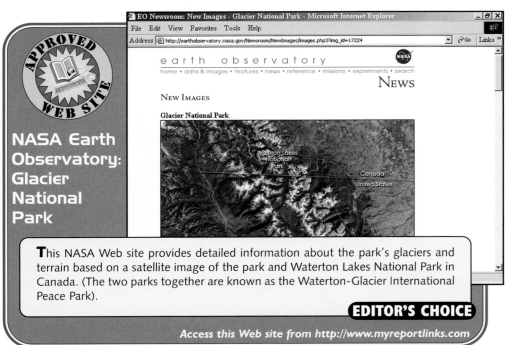

NASA Earth Observatory: Glacier National Park

This NASA Web site provides detailed information about the park's glaciers and terrain based on a satellite image of the park and Waterton Lakes National Park in Canada. (The two parks together are known as the Waterton-Glacier International Peace Park).

EDITOR'S CHOICE

Access this Web site from http://www.myreportlinks.com

water flows into Canada's Saskatchewan River, which pours into the Hudson Bay.

In many mountain areas, water pours right off the cliffs. Two hundred waterfalls add to the sound and beauty of the park. Bird Woman Falls drops nearly five hundred feet (152 meters) from the north slope of Mount Oberlin.

Overall, approximately seven hundred lakes dot Glacier National Park. Most are so small or remote that they have not been named. McDonald, St. Mary, Bowman, and Kintla are the largest lakes. Each of these four is long and narrow and is shaped like a slash. Because Glacier's lakes are so cold, very little plankton is able to grow. This means that the lake waters remain crystal clear.

Indeed, one of Glacier's charms is its pristine quality. Its air and water are among the cleanest and purest in the nation. It is remotely located in northern Montana, the sixth least-populated state. And, as mentioned, it is engulfed by many miles of protected land. Thus, only a small amount of pollution seeps into the park.

⇨ DIVERSE CLIMATES

Throughout the world, people like to boast about how dramatically their weather can change. But the citizens of Browning, Montana, just east of Glacier, have the most remarkable story to tell.

St. Mary Lake is one of the two largest lakes of the seven hundred in the park.

Between January 23 and January 24, 1916, the temperature dropped from 44°F (6.6°C) to −56°F (−49°C). It is the only one-hundred-degree drop within twenty-four hours in recorded history!

At Glacier, wintry conditions last from October to May. When tourists visit during the summer, the weather is typically pleasant. In the higher mountain elevations, it is chilly even in the summer. In fact, snow can fall as late as July.

The climate on Glacier's east side is remarkably different from that on the west. East Glacier has the interior continental climate of the Great Plains. It is warm in the summer—sometimes the temperature reaches the nineties (Fahrenheit) in the valleys—and cold the rest of the year. It is also dry, sunny, and windy. Meanwhile, West Glacier's climate reflects that of the Pacific Northwest. It is cool in the summer but warmer than East Glacier in the winter. It is also cloudier and receives much more rain than the eastern half of the park. Because of the different climates, the plants and wildlife are much different on the two sides.

➡ BOUNTIFUL PLANT LIFE

Viewing Glacier from the distance, one sees only barefaced mountains and greenery below. However, more than a thousand species of plants grow in the Glacier and Waterton Lakes national parks. For a short period during the summer,

Unless you are in the higher elevations, Glacier National Park is usually pleasant during the summer.

colorful wildflowers bloom in Glacier's alpine areas.

The types of plants vary on the west and east sides of the Continental Divide. Because of West Glacier's warm, moist environment, dense forests proliferate. Larch, spruce, fir, hemlock, and lodgepole pine stand tall. Each is noted for its green needles and Christmas-tree shape.

In East Glacier, the flat plains roll up to the mountains. This land is noted for its vibrant flowers. The pasque, lupine, and aster frequently have violet (purple) petals. The gaillardia is shaped like a sunflower, but it is multicolored, such as an orange center with yellow petals.

Indian paintbrush got its name from an American Indian legend. According to the tale, a brave threw down his brushes in frustration while trying to paint a sunset. Indian paint-brush flowers have different

Beargrass is a unique wildflower that grows high in the mountains of the Glacier and Waterton area. Its stalk is several feet high and topped by a white cluster of flowers.

colors, including those that resemble a sunset: orange, red, yellow, and scarlet. Shooting stars also enliven the prairie. These tiny flowers have a yellow base and pinkish red petals.

For about six weeks in July and August, wildflowers flourish high in the mountains. One of the flowers, called beargrass, is the signature plant of the Glacier and Waterton area. This unique wildflower resembles a baseball atop a batting tee. The stalk, which can grow several feet high, is topped by a white flower cluster. This plant blooms only once every several years.

Bright yellow glacier lilies blanket some meadows. Grizzly bears like to feed on them because of their tangy flavor. They will also dig up large areas where glacier lilies grow. The bears feed on the plant's bulbs, which are high in carbohydrates.

Wild blue huckleberries are another favorite of grizzly bears. The calypso orchid, also known as the fairy slipper, is a hard-to-find treasure. Its violet flower resembles a dainty slipper.

ABUNDANT WILDLIFE

Because of its diverse habitats, Glacier is home to many different kinds of animals. More than sixty mammals and more than two hundred and seventy species of birds can be found in the park.

Most of the mammals are little creatures, including rodents, bats, shrews, pikas, rabbits, and hares. These animals, including the rodents, can be cute and amusing. One such rodent, the hoary marmot, has been called a "slinky with fur." The ultra-flexible critter slithers through alpine rock piles. It also emits a distinctive whistling noise when alarmed.

The wandering shrew is only several inches long, even with its long, pointy snout. Constantly looking for food, it eats about eight times its body weight every day. The northern flying squirrel must be seen to be believed. Though it looks like a common squirrel when it climbs a tree, it can

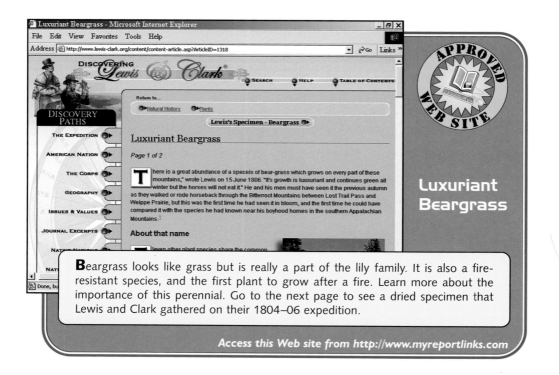

Beargrass looks like grass but is really a part of the lily family. It is also a fire-resistant species, and the first plant to grow after a fire. Learn more about the importance of this perennial. Go to the next page to see a dried specimen that Lewis and Clark gathered on their 1804–06 expedition.

Access this Web site from http://www.myreportlinks.com

actually fly—or, more accurately, glide—up to thirty yards (27.4 meters). When it spreads its limbs, its loose skin stretches out like the wings of a hang glider.

⊖ THE GRIZZLY

Many thousands of grizzly bears once foraged in North America's wilderness, but today only about nine hundred live on the continent. Approximately three hundred of them are in Glacier National Park. Grizzlies are much more imposing than black bears, eight hundred of which roam the park. Adult grizzlies typically weigh three hundred to six hundred pounds (136 to 272 kilograms), with a few at more than a thousand pounds (453 kilograms). In comparison, the average adult black bear weighs a modest 220 pounds (100 kilograms). The Blackfeet referred to the grizzly as "real bear."

Despite the grizzlies' great size, tourists rarely get to see this mighty creature. These animals live in remote areas of the park, where they forage on plants, rodents, and animal carcasses. At Glacier, park rangers educate visitors about how to avoid grizzlies. Those who think they can outrun these massive mammals are sadly mistaken. A grizzly can speed along at thirty mph (48.3 kmph)—and run the sixty-yard dash in about four seconds!

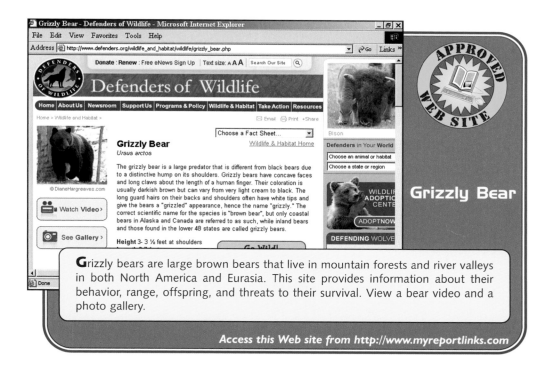

Grizzly bears are large brown bears that live in mountain forests and river valleys in both North America and Eurasia. This site provides information about their behavior, range, offspring, and threats to their survival. View a bear video and a photo gallery.

Access this Web site from http://www.myreportlinks.com

➡ A VARIETY OF MAMMALS

When James J. Hill ran the Great Northern Railway to the Glacier region, he made sure that the mountain goat was pictured on the trains. Those who drive down Going-to-the-Sun Road often pull over to witness this amazing creature. The mountain goat is actually a species of mountain antelope. It lives on the mountains' high, steep cliffs so as to avoid other animals. The mountain goat's hooves have rubbery pads, which provide extraordinary traction. The broad-shouldered animal also has exceptional balance and strength for climbing. Its thick, rough fur protects the mountain goat against the cold mountain winds.

The Rocky Mountain sheep, also called the bighorn sheep, is another visitor favorite. This large ungulate, or hoofed animal, lives in the mountains' high valleys, slopes, and cliffs. It is also known as the bighorn sheep. The male has curled

▲ *A small herd of bighorn sheep rams racing across a snowy alpine meadow above Logan Pass.*

horns that weigh about thirty pounds. In autumn, males try to establish dominance by crashing horns with their rivals. The loud, hollow sound can be heard through much of the park.

Thousands of mule and white-tailed deer trot through Glacier National Park. The two animals look similar, but "mulies" have bigger bodies and larger ears. Elk are larger "cousins" of the deer, but they are hard to spot. During the summer, they stay in high-elevation mountain meadows. In autumn during mating season, the male elk makes his bugle call, which sounds like a high-pitched flute.

The number of gray wolves at Glacier dwindled in the early 1900s. The fearsome predators, however, have made a comeback and were recently removed from the endangered species list.[1] Gray wolves are wary of people, so few visitors ever get to see them. In the evenings, they make their presence known when they howl at the moon.

While bison and woodland caribou once lived in the Glacier region, those animals are no longer present in the park. Other large mammals that do live in Glacier include moose, coyotes, Canadian lynx, and mountain lions. The lynx and lions are small in numbers and rarely seen by tourists. Other mammals of note include wolverines, badgers, beavers, river otters, porcupines, and mink.

➲ WINGED WONDERS

Nothing is more American than a bald eagle—
the national bird—flying above the Continental
Divide. Some visitors to Glacier are fortunate to
witness such a spine-tingling moment. These
white-headed, fierce-looking birds possess wing-
spans as wide as six feet (1.8 meters). Bald eagles

▲ Harlequin ducks, known for their unusual colors, prefer to live in the
rapid mountain streams of the park.

hover above Glacier's lakes and river, where they prey on fish and other small animals.

Each spring, local Montanans visit Glacier to watch the peculiar harlequin ducks. The colors on the female are subdued browns. But the male's splashy colors, wrote Gary Turback of *National Wildlife*, are "seemingly assembled by a committee of first graders."[2] These ducks are unusual in that they migrate east and west as opposed to north and south. They also prefer to live in rapid mountain streams rather than calm marshes. Onlookers chuckle while watching the harlequins trying to maneuver the roaring rapids.

Two hundred and sixty species of birds in all have been documented in Glacier National Park. Hawks, osprey, golden eagles, and great horned owls nest in this region. The pale blue Clark's nutcracker is a favorite of bird-watchers, but its numbers in the park are declining due to the reduction of whitebark pines. Waterfowl, meaning those birds that swim and live near the water, include the great blue heron, tundra swan, American wigeon, and Canada goose.

REPTILES AND AMPHIBIANS

Visitors are hard-pressed to find a reptile in this frigid climate, but they do exist. Garter snakes and the western painted turtle continue to brave the elements. The frequently seen western spotted frog heads the list of amphibians at Glacier. Others include the long-toed salamander, western toad, tailed frog, and Pacific tree frog. Park officials take even the smallest animals seriously. After a large fire in 2001, they closed some roads the following year so that western toads could safely migrate across them to other areas.

⊖ PRESERVING THE ECOSYSTEM

Glacier's climates, plant life, and wildlife are diverse, but they are all part of the same eco-system, or ecological system. This system, often referred to as the "Crown of the Continent Ecosystem," encompasses sixteen thousand square miles (41,440 square kilometers). In recent decades, scientists have learned the importance of keeping ecosystems intact as much as possible. Disruptions could lead to a chain reaction of neg-ative effects.

Even a microscopic organism can create an ecological catastrophe. For example, the tiny, non-native mud snail has caused problems in several western states. Mud snails crowd out communities of aquatic insects, which are a primary food source for fish. Mud snails also consume waters' algae growth—another main food source for fish. If fish starve, then animals that feed on fish also go hungry. Other factors that can corrupt an ecosystem are hunting, irresponsible human behavior, and pollution.

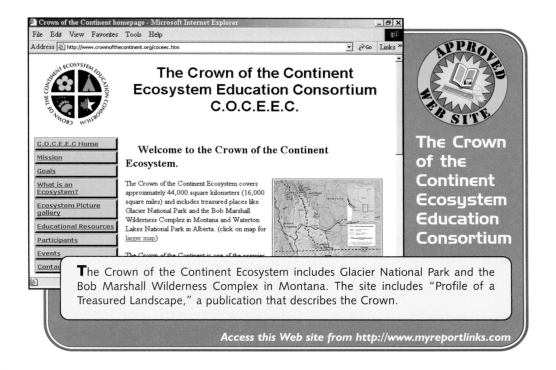

The Crown of the Continent Ecosystem includes Glacier National Park and the Bob Marshall Wilderness Complex in Montana. The site includes "Profile of a Treasured Landscape," a publication that describes the Crown.

Access this Web site from http://www.myreportlinks.com

The Crown of the Continent Ecosystem is the most pristine in the continental United States. The region's remote location as well as excellent preservation efforts have helped keep the ecosystem intact. However, maintaining such purity while hosting close to 2 million visitors per year is no easy task. Park officials address ecological concerns on a daily basis, as the next chapter explains.

Chapter 5

Mountains topped with glaciers surround Alpine Lake. Global warming poses a constant threat to the park's glaciers.

Threats to the Park

In nearly a century of existence, Glacier National Park has remained virtually pure. However, Glacier currently faces a large number of threats—more than at most national parks. Said conservationist Steve Thompson, "If this keeps up, we may be looking at the National Park Formerly Known as Glacier."[1] The park is actually one of twelve national parks that face great risks, according to a report by the National Resources Defense Council and The Rocky Mountain Climate Organization.

First of all, Glacier is being disturbed by the same factors that are affecting America's national parks in general. The nation's swelling population, much of which is occurring in the West, is one such factor.

More hotels, restaurants, stores, and vacation homes are being built near national parks. This leads to more pollution, which affects both plants and animals. Moreover, the poorly designed night-time lights that surround the parks have caused campers to not enjoy starry nights as they once did.

In addition, attendance at national parks has skyrocketed in recent decades. The noise, car fumes, and other forms of invasiveness disturb the parks' ecosystems. Vehicles and people drag nonnative plants, insects, and other organisms into the parks. Such intrusions have affected more than two million acres of national parkland and are destroying natural resources. Finally,

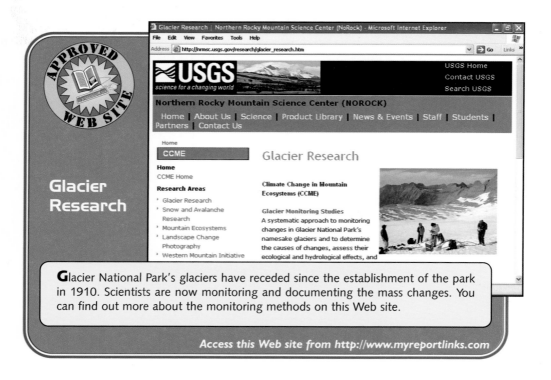

Glacier National Park's glaciers have receded since the establishment of the park in 1910. Scientists are now monitoring and documenting the mass changes. You can find out more about the monitoring methods on this Web site.

Access this Web site from http://www.myreportlinks.com

global warming is having widespread effects on America's wilderness—effects that could become devastating.

Glacier, of course, faces its own specific problems. Some of the major concerns currently facing park officials are detailed next.

⮕POPULATION AND POLLUTION

Flathead Valley, west of the park, is known as the "Gateway to Glacier." Once a remote location, it now caters to tourists. Thousands come to enjoy skiing, shopping, fine dining, and championship level golf courses. "I wouldn't drive up the Flathead Valley again," wrote a visitor. "You know . . . there's too much sprawl. It looks too much like California."[2]

According to a 2007 article in The *New York Times*, Flathead County, on the western edge of Glacier, has experienced a 44 percent population boom since 1990.[3] Subdivisions, vacation homes, and large chain stores are being built close to the park's western border. Flathead Valley's Kalispell is the largest city in northwest Montana; its population increased from 14,000 in 2000 to 17,000 in 2004. The resulting pollution in Flathead Valley affects the park.

Meanwhile, Glacier is also affected by air pollution not related to the local population. Like other parks in America's interior West, it has been experiencing increasing levels of ammonium, nitrates, and ozone. These pollutants, largely caused by the booming oil and gas industry in the West, have caused a haze to hover over Glacier.

The parks in the interior West are experiencing high levels of nitrogen deposition, which is dangerous. Too much nitrogen encourages the growth of grasses and sedges. These plants prevent the growth of wildflowers vital to the parks' ecosystems. Various agencies are working to try to regulate these emissions. "We can turn this boat around, because we caught it before it went too far," says Karl Cordova, a biologist at Rocky Mountain National Park. "Working together, we can make things happen."[4]

COAL IN CANADA

Just north of the Canadian border, at the headwaters of the North Fork of the Flathead River, lay enormous deposits of coal. In 2007, the Toronto-based Cline Mining Corporation sought to establish a coal mine there. Residents of northern Montana balked at the idea. "Let's not mince words or understate the threat this mine poses to our water, wildlife and way of life," wrote conservationist Dave Hadden, president of the Flathead Coalition. "If the Cline mine proceeds we Montanans, sooner or later, will have a mess on our hands."[5]

According to the opponents of the project, emissions from the coal excavation would pollute the air and water of Glacier National Park. Potential pollutants include nitrates, nitrites, and the toxic element selenium. Wrote Hadden: "[W]e'll have fewer, if any bull trout; wildlife habitat and wildlife migration routes will be seriously compromised or destroyed; Glacier National Park's western boundary and Flathead Lake will receive all that toxic water."[6] Environmental groups and Montana state leaders have vowed to resist the proposed project to the bitter end.

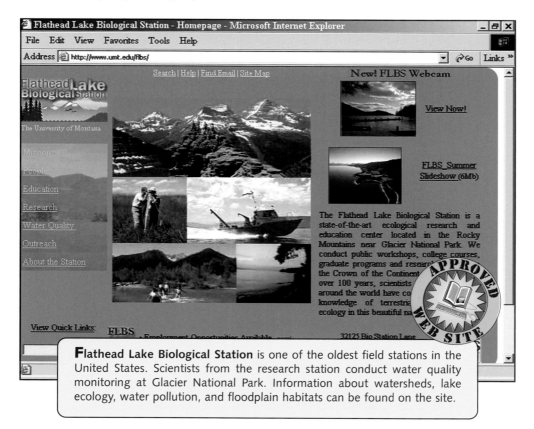

Flathead Lake Biological Station is one of the oldest field stations in the United States. Scientists from the research station conduct water quality monitoring at Glacier National Park. Information about watersheds, lake ecology, water pollution, and floodplain habitats can be found on the site.

⊜ FISH AT RISK

The bull trout and grizzly bear have long been symbolic animals of Glacier National Park. However, the future of each is in jeopardy.

For many years, nonnative lake trout were added to the waters of Glacier. This introduction spelled doom for the native bull trout. The lake trout ate the bull trout, whose numbers gradually diminished. In 1998, the U.S. Fish and Wildlife Service listed the bull trout as "threat-ened." "There's an awful lot of people who feel very sad, very bad

Approximately three hundred grizzly ▷ bears like this one live in the remote areas of Glacier National Park. Adult grizzlies are massive animals, typically weighing from three hundred to six hundred pounds.

that it was a native fish of Montana," said Fay Eklund. "*Was* a native fish of Montana."[7]

Park officials have ended the practice of planting nonnative fish in Glacier. Moreover, it is illegal

to catch and keep a bull trout in the park's lakes, rivers, and streams. Currently, the National Park Service is exploring ways to reestablish native fish in some of the park's waters.

BEAR ATTACKS

For the entire history of Glacier National Park, bears have always posed a danger to visitors. Grizzlies roam many areas of the park. They are frequently spotted in Many Glacier Valley, around Huckleberry Mountain, and in the Logan Pass Area. Though grizzlies are much bigger, faster, and stronger than humans, they tend to shy away from people. Nevertheless, they occasionally attack. An average of one or two bear attacks are reported at Glacier each year.

The National Park Service offers many tips on bear safety. It recommends that before hiking, visitors should stop at a visitor center or ranger station to get an update on bear activity in the area. They should hike in groups of three or more. Hikers should not hike alone, because they have the greatest chance of encountering a bear when on their own. Hiking at dusk and dawn, when bears are active, should be avoided, and people should not enter any closed trails. (Trails are usually closed because bears were sighted there.)

Bears should be observed only from a distance, and people should not approach a bear to take its

▲ A view of conifers—trees that produce seeds in cones—in the park. Whitebark pines are a type of conifer tree threatened by blister rust, a nonnative fungus.

photo or feed a bear under any circumstances. Camps should be kept clean, since bears are attracted to whatever is edible. Food, dirty dishes, and even toiletries need to be stored in a closed vehicle or food locker, and garbage must be tossed into bear-proof garbage cans. These are not recommendations, but park requirements.

Visitors must also take care to stay away from a bear's cubs and food. Otherwise, an adult bear will consider them a threat. If you do have a close encounter with a bear, stay calm, talk softly, avoid eye contact, and slowly back away. Do not run or scream, for such behavior could provoke a bear to chase you. And don't even consider climbing a tree, for bears are agile and are much better climbers than people.

⮞WHITEBARKS AND BLISTER RUST

Since the early 1900s, a nonnative fungus called blister rust has been killing Glacier's whitebark pine trees. Blister rust is wreaking havoc in many areas of the country, but its effects are particularly severe at Glacier National Park. It is estimated that almost 90 percent of the park's whitebark pines have died.

Glacier cannot afford to lose its whitebark pines. These trees, which grow high in the mountains, produce cones that contain pine seeds. These seeds are high in fat and are an important food source for many animals. Most of the seeds are harvested by the Clark's nutcracker (a bird) and the red squirrel. Each of these animals transports the seeds to caches, or little storage areas.

Grizzly and black bears inevitably raid these caches from August to late fall and into the spring. Pine nuts, in fact, are a large part of a bear's diet. Should these nuts become unavailable, bears would have to roam to lower elevations to forage for food. That would make them a greater threat to people.

The whitebark trees themselves are also important. With their large trunks, they provide good nesting areas for squirrels and birds. They also grow at higher elevation than other trees, and

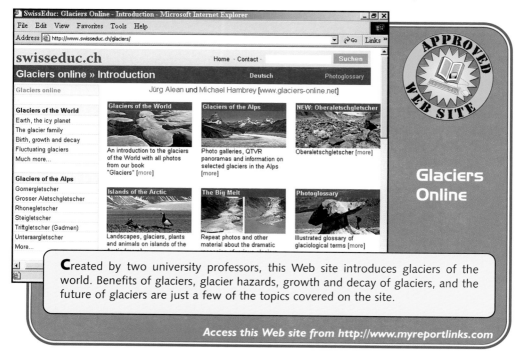

Created by two university professors, this Web site introduces glaciers of the world. Benefits of glaciers, glacier hazards, growth and decay of glaciers, and the future of glaciers are just a few of the topics covered on the site.

Access this Web site from http://www.myreportlinks.com

their presence allows other trees to grow below. Finally, their large branches capture the northern snow. This delays the melting of snow and extends the flow periods for streams.

From 1930 to 1970, efforts were made at Glacier to control the spread of blister rust. Unfortunately, the efforts were not successful. In the early 2000s, a new plan was developed. Thousands of blister rust-resistant whitebark pine tree seedlings were planted. Research by the USDA Forest Service indicated that this variety of young trees had natural genetic resistance to the rust. The results have appeared promising, but the study of this restoration program is not over.

MELTING GLACIERS

All across the world, people are concerned about global warming. The average worldwide temperature has risen—and it will continue to rise in the future. Some scientists claim that the sun's temperature fluctuates, and it is currently getting warmer. But the rise in carbon dioxide is also a significant factor. This gas is emitted by the burning of coal, oil, and natural gas. As the world becomes more industrialized, and as more people drive cars, even more carbon dioxide is created. Carbon dioxide and other gases create a "greenhouse effect." This means that the gases hover in the

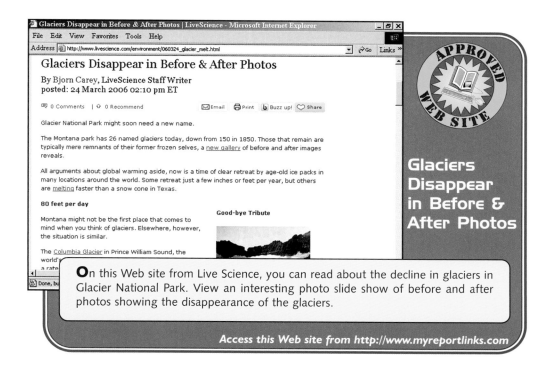

Glaciers Disappear in Before & After Photos

By Bjorn Carey, LiveScience Staff Writer
posted: 24 March 2006 02:10 pm ET

0 Comments | 0 Recommend   Email   Print   Buzz up!   Share

Glacier National Park might soon need a new name.

The Montana park has 26 named glaciers today, down from 150 in 1850. Those that remain are typically mere remnants of their former frozen selves, a new gallery of before and after images reveals.

All arguments about global warming aside, now is a time of clear retreat by age-old ice packs in many locations around the world. Some retreat just a few inches or feet per year, but others are melting faster than a snow cone in Texas.

80 feet per day

Montana might not be the first place that comes to mind when you think of glaciers. Elsewhere, however, the situation is similar.

Good-bye Tribute

The Columbia Glacier in Prince William Sound, the world's
a rate

Glaciers Disappear in Before & After Photos

On this Web site from Live Science, you can read about the decline in glaciers in Glacier National Park. View an interesting photo slide show of before and after photos showing the disappearance of the glaciers.

Access this Web site from http://www.myreportlinks.com

atmosphere and prevent heat from escaping. Thus, the world gets warmer.

Significant global warming would lead to dramatic changes. Polar ice caps will continue to melt, causing sea levels to rise. This water will pour onto the continents' shores, causing developed areas to be washed away. Global warming could also increase extreme weather events (such as hurricanes) and expand the range of tropical diseases and insect pests.

Glacier National Park is among the areas already feeling the effects of global warming. Since 1910, the average summertime temperature at Glacier has risen three degrees. Consequently,

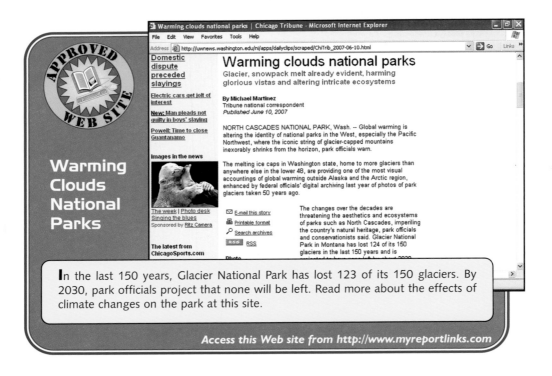

Warming clouds national parks | Chicago Tribune - Microsoft Internet Explorer

File   Edit   View   Favorites   Tools   Help

Address http://uwnews.washington.edu/ni/apps/dailyclips/scraped/ChiTrib_2007-06-10.html   Go   Links

Domestic
dispute
preceded
slayings

Electric cars get jolt of
interest

New: Man pleads not
guilty in boys' slaying

Powell: Time to close
Guantanamo

Images in the news

The week | Photo desk
Singing the blues
Sponsored by Ritz Camera

The latest from
ChicagoSports.com

Warming clouds national parks

Glacier, snowpack melt already evident, harming
glorious vistas and altering intricate ecosystems

By Michael Martinez
Tribune national correspondent
Published June 10, 2007

NORTH CASCADES NATIONAL PARK, Wash. -- Global warming is
altering the identity of national parks in the West, especially the Pacific
Northwest, where the iconic string of glacier-capped mountains
inexorably shrinks from the horizon, park officials warn.

The melting ice caps in Washington state, home to more glaciers than
anywhere else in the lower 48, are providing one of the most visual
accountings of global warming outside Alaska and the Arctic region,
enhanced by federal officials' digital archiving last year of photos of park
glaciers taken 50 years ago.

The changes over the decades are
threatening the aesthetics and ecosystems
of parks such as North Cascades, imperiling
the country's natural heritage, park officials
and conservationists said. Glacier National
Park in Montana has lost 124 of its 150
glaciers in the last 150 years and is

E-mail this story

Printable format

Search archives

RSS   RSS

Photo

**Warming
Clouds
National
Parks**

In the last 150 years, Glacier National Park has lost 123 of its 150 glaciers. By 2030, park officials project that none will be left. Read more about the effects of climate changes on the park at this site.

Access this Web site from http://www.myreportlinks.com

the glaciers have melted at a rapid pace. More than one hundred have disappeared over the last one hundred and fifty years. Since the late 1960s, the warming trend has worsened. If nothing is done to curb global warming, scientists predict that all of the twenty-seven remaining glaciers in the park will completely melt by 2030.

The diminished glaciers will in turn affect the wildlife in the park. For example, avalanches from the glaciers have torn down trees in the park. With trees out of the way, berry bushes have had a chance to grow. Bears at Glacier have relied heavily on berries for food. Fewer glaciers will lead to fewer avalanches, which in turn will lead to fewer berry bushes. And fewer berry bushes will lead to fewer bears. Without glaciers, other species of animals will either die out or migrate out of the park for good.

Sadly, little can be done to stop the melting. It will take many years or decades—if it's possible at all—for the international community to curtail global warming. Scientists predict that even if the region's temperature remains constant from now on, all of the park's glaciers likely will still be gone by the year 2100.

Chapter

6

REC SEARCH   FOCUS   NIGHT M

CARD

DIGITAL

ON/OFF

Hikers atop Abbott Ridge in Glacier National Park.

Exploring Glacier

Montana's population is less than one million. But each year, close to 2 million people visit Glacier National Park. Tourists come from hundreds, even thousands, of miles away to experience the park's extraordinary wonders.

➔ HOW TO GET THERE

Glacier National Park is not easy to reach. Airfare to Glacier Park International Airport in nearby Kalispell, Montana, is typically expensive, and so are the flights to the airports in Great Falls and Missoula, Montana. Moreover, those two airports are more than one hundred and fifty miles from the park. Some long-distance commuters prefer to take the train to Glacier. Amtrak stops outside West Glacier and, in the summer only, East Glacier.

Motorists can access either the east or west sides of Glacier by taking U.S. Highway 2, while Highway 89 runs north and south along the eastern boundary of the park. The park is open year-round, twenty-four hours a day. However, many roads are closed due to snow in the fall, winter, and spring. While transportation might be expensive, admission to the park is a bargain. A vehicle's passengers can stay in the park for seven days for an admission fee of just twenty-five dollars.

First-time tourists may want to check out the visitor centers, which are located in Apgar, Logan

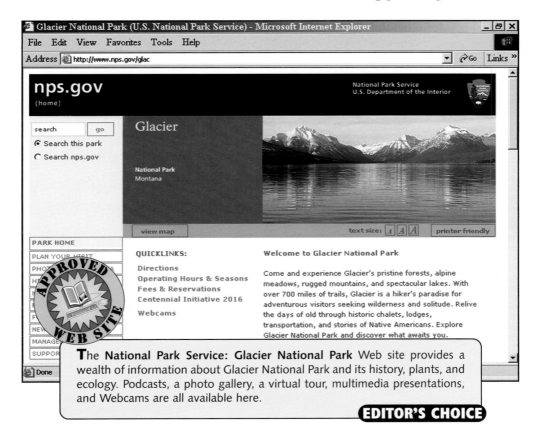

The **National Park Service: Glacier National Park** Web site provides a wealth of information about Glacier National Park and its history, plants, and ecology. Podcasts, a photo gallery, a virtual tour, multimedia presentations, and Webcams are all available here.

EDITOR'S CHOICE

Pass, and St. Mary. Park rangers are eager to answer questions and provide information.

→ ORIENT YOURSELF

Before exploring Glacier National Park, it is best to get oriented. The park is comprised of multiple areas, eight of which are described below. Most of these areas lie just inside the park's western, southern, and eastern borders.

• Lake McDonald: Glacier's largest lake is located next to the West Entrance Station. The city of West Glacier is adjacent to this entrance, while Apgar Village rests in the park on the shores of Lake McDonald. The western side of Going-to-the-Sun Road begins here.

• Polebridge: This small community rests on the west edge of the park, twenty miles north of the Lake McDonald area. Surrounded by mountains on the east and west, it is tucked into the North Fork Flathead River valley.

• Walton: This remote valley sits near the southern tip of Glacier National Park. It is just north of Essex, Montana (population: thirty).

• Two Medicine Lake: The Two Medicine Lake area, located in the southeast corner of the park, may have the best vistas in all of Glacier. It lies just west of a Montana town called East Glacier Park, where Amtrak passengers arrive.

Glacier National Park Pictures - US National Parks stock photos, fine art prints by QTL - Microsoft Inter... _ 🗗 ✕

File   Edit   View   Favorites   Tools   Help

Address http://www.terragalleria.com/parks/np.glacier.html   ⟳Go Links »

Glacier National Park

Pictures by QT Luong

[1 : Overview][2 : Going-to-the-Sun West] [3 : Logan Pass] [4 : East] [5 : Many Glacier]
[6 : Grinnell Lake and Trail] [7 : Grinnell Glacier] [8 : Wildlife] [9 : People] [All]

View only Large Format photographs of Glacier National Park

[Click on any picture to see a larger image and details, to add to selection, to order, and to download wallpaper.]

Logan Pass, wildlife, Grinnell Lake, trees, wildflowers, icebergs, and mountains are featured in these photographs of **Glacier National Park**.

• Cut Bank: This is shorthand for the North Fork Cut Bank Creek Valley. It rests inside Glacier's east border, a few miles north of Two Medicine Lake.

• St. Mary: This name refers to the town along Glacier's eastern border. In the same area rests St. Mary Lake, Lower St. Mary Lake, St. Mary River, and St. Mary Valley. The eastern side of Going-to-the-Sun Road begins here.

• Logan Pass: In the exact center of the park, Logan Pass is the highest point on Going-to-the-

A summertime view of Two Medicine Lake in the southeast corner of the park.

Sun Road at 6,680 feet (2,036 meters). Many drivers park here and enjoy the glorious views.

• Many Glacier: This area sits in the northeast region of the park. It encompasses fifteen lakes as well as meadows and glaciers.

⊜ THE MAIN ROAD

A large percentage of Glacier National Park visitors simply drive right through the park. But what

a ride! Going-to-the-Sun Road ranks among the best scenic drives in North America. As Montana governor Frank H. Cooney said in 1933, "There is no highway which will give the seer, the lover of grandeur of the Creator's handiwork, more thrills, more genuine satisfaction deep in his being, than will a trip over this road."[1]

This two-lane roadway bisects the park, and is fifty-two miles (83.7 kilometers) in all. From east to west, it stretches across every type of terrain that Glacier provides. Motorists drive past glacial lakes in the valleys before ascending more than a mile above sea level. At one point, the road emerges from forest and offers an up-close view of Glacier's mountain peaks. Particularly impressive are Mount Siyeh at 10,014 feet (3,052 meters) and Going-to-the-Sun Mountain at 9,642 feet (2,939 meters).

Logan Pass, the highest point on Going-to-the-Sun Road at 6,680 feet (2,036 meters).

At various points on Going-to-the-Sun Road, visitors can park their vehicles and walk around. Many are wowed by the vibrant wildflower meadows and the magnificent alpine vistas. Others try to spot a mountain goat, bighorn sheep, or other distinctive animal. In the west, many a moose turns out at the appropriately named Moose Turnout.

A SIGHTSEER'S PARADISE

Going-to-the-Sun Road attracts the tourists, but Glacier National Park has so much more to see. The Garden Wall, on the west side of the Continental Divide, is one of Glacier's must-see attractions. The Garden Wall is a "rock spine" formed by glaciers. It includes the Weeping Wall, where water pours to the roadway below. The drive up to Many Glacier Valley pays off in abundance. There you will find a meadow surrounded by mountainsides and high rock faces. Animals love this area, including Glacier's mountain goats.

The mountain goats like to eat salt, and they find plenty of it on a steep bank of the Flathead River. These animals used to cross U.S. Highway 2 to reach the "salt lick," but they were always in danger of being hit by cars. To help them, in the late 1970s, the Federal Highway Administration constructed a tunnel under the highway that the goats could walk through. In addition, the

National Park Service built the Goat Lick Overlook for visitors to view the animals enjoying their snack.

Goose Island View is a favorite of photographers. There, cameras capture blue sky, mountain peaks, flowered terrain, St. Mary Lake, and Wild Goose Island. Glacier boasts scores of waterfalls, including some that run off near Going-to-the-Sun Road. Many others are tucked away in the mountains but may be worth the hike to get there. Each of the falls is unique. Silver Staircase Falls flows down a staircase of rocks. Roadside Falls trickles down a long dirt ditch. Running Eagle Falls emerges from a tunnel of rock.

It is not hard to spot Mount Reynolds. Glaciers sharpened this mountain like a pencil, creating a pyramid-shaped peak, also known as a glacial horn. Tourists find tranquility among Glacier's many lakes. Lake McDonald, St. Mary Lake, and Swiftcurrent Lake rank among the favorite destinations.

COLORFUL FLORA

Some tourists visit Glacier just for the flowers. Wildflowers begin to bloom in the valleys in the late spring. The Logan Pass area erupts with alpine wildflowers from late June to early August. Huckleberries, which grow on both sides of Glacier, are one of the perks of the park. Glacier

officials allow each visitor to collect one quart of
huckleberries per day.
People eat them as is or
use them to make jam,
pies, and other tasty
treats—even huckleberry
soda!

TAKE A HIKE

More than half of Glacier
National Park's visitors
go on a hike. Park offi-
cials accommodate these
eager explorers with
more than 730 miles
(1,175 kilometers) of
hiking trails. Most go on
a short hike or an all-day
hike. Others obtain a
permit for backcountry
camping and hiking.

Some of the hikes are
short with little elevation
change, while others
require walks up steep
terrain. In the valleys,
trails are dry enough
for hiking by about

Wild Goose Island, in the center of St. Mary Lake, is a favorite scene captured by photographers.

mid-June. But those who want to hike on the high-elevation trails typically have to wait until late July before they are free of snow. Trails.com has selected the park's "Best Easy Day Hikes."[2] Of these, it gives five stars (out of five) to the following:

• Grinnell Lake: On this six-mile (9.6-kilometer) trail, you'll witness sparkling mountain lakes and have the chance to stand on a glacier. The trail ends at Upper Grinnell Lake and Grinnell Glacier, which is at the base of the Continental Divide.

• Haystack Butte: This may be the best section of the popular Highline Trail. While meandering along the west face of the Continental Divide, the trail offers outstanding opportunities for wildlife viewing. Look for hoary marmots and pikas, mountain goats and bighorn sheep. Raptors often soar above.

• Trail of the Cedars: This 0.8-mile (1.3-kilometer)loop trail is perfect if you're looking for a great short hike. The trail winds past "weeping" rocks and through a garden of ferns. Nearly half of the path is on a boardwalk. This is the only trail that is completely wheelchair accessible.

Of course, every trail in Glacier offers glorious views, from wildflowers and waterfalls to glaciers and mountaintops. Popular trails include Apgar Lookout, Cut Bank Creek, Gunsight Pass, the Belly River Trail, the Garden Wall, and the Snowshoe

Trail. Dick Honrath, who has traversed Glacier's trails for twenty-five years, prefers the high-altitude trail between Dawson Pass and Mount Morgan. "Nothing but peak upon peak," he described. "You're on top of the world."[3]

Before hitting the trails, you must gear up for the challenge. First of all, hiking boots are essential. They not only give you good traction on the rocky terrain, but they also provide full ankle support. Sneaker wearers often end up twisting an ankle.

Weather can change dramatically at Glacier, and winds can blow ferociously. Moreover, it gets colder the higher you climb. Thus, proper dress and supplies are essential. A day hiker's supply list should include a well-insulated jacket, a rain/wind jacket, a first-aid kit, food, and an ample supply of water. Do not plan on drinking the water of Glacier's lakes and streams. Although it may look crystal clear, it is untreated and could be contaminated with giardia. This tiny parasite can cause gastrointestinal illness.

CAMPING OUT

Although Glacier National Park attracts masses of sightseers and hikers, only a small percentage of them camp out in the park. The weather has much to do with this; the daytime temperatures are pleasant during the summer, but the nights are

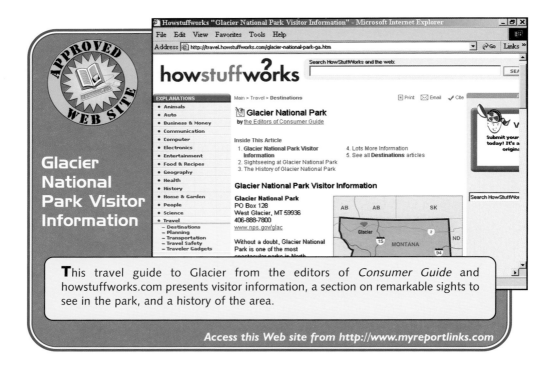

This travel guide to Glacier from the editors of *Consumer Guide* and howstuffworks.com presents visitor information, a section on remarkable sights to see in the park, and a history of the area.

Access this Web site from http://www.myreportlinks.com

always cold. Even in July, it often gets close to freezing in the early hours of the morning.

If you can find a way to keep warm, camping in the Rocky Mountains can be a heavenly experience. You can fill your days with hiking, fishing, or simply reading a book. In the evenings, you can enjoy a flame-cooked dinner, roasted marshmallows, spooky stories, or sing-alongs. At night, you're alone with your deepest thoughts underneath a canopy of stars.

Glacier National Park includes ten major campgrounds, each of varying sizes. Apgar has 196 campsites and is the largest, followed by Fish

Creek with 180, St. Mary with 148, and Many Glacier with 110. You can make reservations at Fish Creek and St. Mary, but everywhere else is on a first come/first serve basis only. Fees range from $10 to $23 per vehicle.

➡ ROUGHING IT

In July and August, campgrounds tend to fill up before noon, so it is best to arrive early. The Apgar and St. Mary campgrounds are open year-round for "primitive camping." Glacier also includes sixty-six backcountry sites for backpackers. All of these are small, with only two to seven campsites each.

Do not expect deluxe accommodations at any of the campgrounds. The larger ones provide restrooms with flush toilets and cold running water. However, most of the campgrounds do not offer shower or laundry facilities. Besides the cold nights, you must prepare for weather changes throughout the day. At Glacier, storms can strike suddenly, soaking vacationers' camping and sleeping gear.

As mentioned in chapter 5, campers must put all food left after meals in bear-proof trash cans to avoid attracting bears. Campers also need to wash their dishes and utensils and clean the stove and fire grill. Campers are urged to take even further precautions: "Packs, sleeping bags, and clothes should be kept free of food odors," a Web site advising campers states. "As a precaution against the presence of food odors, wash your hands and face before retiring. If possible, do not sleep in clothes worn while cooking."[4] Soaps, lotions, and other scented items might also attract bears.

Mountain lions are another potential threat. Though rare, attacks have occurred in recent years. Mountain lions are more likely to go after animals, so if you bring a pet, do not leave it unattended.

⮕ FUN IN THE WATER

On a warm, sunshiny day, you might be tempted to dive into Glacier's sparkling lakes. But don't be fooled. Even in August, the waters are generally too cold for swimming. The one exception to this is Lake McDonald, which is located on the west side of the park. That lake soaks up the warm afternoon sun during the summer and reaches temperatures in the low 70s, so many visitors are able to swim there.

Boating is a favorite pastime, and visitors are welcome to bring their motorboats and sailboats to Glacier's lakes. Tourists also can rent boats at several locations. Water skiing is allowed (with many restrictions), but jet skiing is prohibited. Like natives or explorers from an earlier time, visitors can slide down rivers and streams in canoes.

Thrill seekers can enjoy white-water rafting on the Flathead River.

The park has many regulations concerning boating. You can check out Glacier's visitor centers or its official Web site for more information.

⇨ Go Fish

At one time, Glacier National Park catered to the needs and enjoyment of visiting fishermen. The National Park Service even planted exotic game fish in Glacier's waters to fulfill that aim. But in recent decades, the park's ecosystem has been the number one priority. Regarding fishing, one of the park's objectives is to "maintain natural aquatic

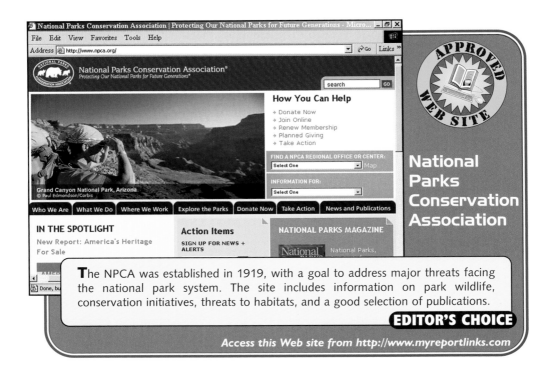

The NPCA was established in 1919, with a goal to address major threats facing the national park system. The site includes information on park wildlife, conservation initiatives, threats to habitats, and a good selection of publications.

EDITOR'S CHOICE

Access this Web site from http://www.myreportlinks.com

environments as they would now exist if modern man had not interfered."[5]

Visitors can enjoy a wonderful fishing trip to Glacier, but they must follow the park's strict regulations. As mentioned, catching and possessing the threatened bull trout is prohibited. In addition, you can catch and keep only two cutthroat trout and no more than five of the following: burbot, northern pike, whitefish, kokanee salmon, brook trout, grayling, rainbow trout, and lake trout.

The park's literature and Web site discuss where and when you can fish, what kinds of equipment and bait are allowed, and how you should dispose of the entrails. They even discuss how to catch and release the fish.

Glacier is not known for its big fish, and sometimes it seems that the fish are not biting at all. Stream fishing is particularly challenging. Visitors have better luck on the lakes, especially Elizabeth, Ellen Wilson, Hidden, Grace, Avalanche, and Isabel.

BIKERS WELCOME

Bicyclists are well received at Glacier National Park, especially since bikes are eco-friendly. In fact, while those in motor vehicles must pay $25 for a seven-day pass, those arriving on bicycle are admitted for just $12. With some exceptions,

A snowplow works on Going-to-the-Sun Road after a heavy snowfall.

bikers can share the roads with cars and trucks. Bicycles are not allowed on trails, except for the hiker/biker trail from Apgar to West Glacier—a paved trail that stretches two miles. Visitors can rent bikes in neighboring communities, but not in the park.

⊖WINTER WONDERLAND

While debates about snowmobile usage rage in Yellowstone National Park, at Glacier this is not an issue. The machines are not permitted anywhere in the park. Nevertheless, tourists can enjoy other winter sports within Glacier's borders.

Of course, "winter" in this region extends from fall to spring. In the dead of winter, it is often too cold and windy in East Glacier to enjoy outdoor activities. Visitors are better off in West Glacier, where the daytime temperatures usually hover in the teens and twenties.

Both in and around Glacier, people enjoy snowboarding, snowshoeing, and skiing—both downhill and cross-country. Big Mountain Resort in Flathead Valley offers groomed trails and deluxe accommodations. Conversely, skiers in the park are largely on their own. Visitors can ski on trails and in other areas, but at their own risk. Park literature discusses all the potential dangers and how to avoid them. Risks include getting lost, hypothermia, frostbite, avalanches, falling through ice, tumbling down mountains, and being attacked by animals! Skiers who are unfamiliar with the park should stick to the safe trails.

→ WHERE TO STAY

If you don't want to "rough it" in Glacier's campgrounds, you can still spend your nights within the park's borders. Glacier offers a variety of lodging, from deluxe hotels to lonesome chalets. Those who are planning a summer vacation should try to make reservations at least six months in advance.

National Park Service: Architecture in the Parks (Great Northern Railway Buildings) - Microsoft Internet...

File   Edit   View   Favorites   Tools   Help

Address http://www.nps.gov/history/history/online_books/harrison/harrison8.htm   Go   Links »

on-line book

Architecture in the Parks

A National Historic Landmark Theme Study

Architecture in the Parks
National Historic Landmark
Theme Study

Cover Page

MENU

Contents

Introductory Essay

Many Glacier Hotel
Glacier National Park
Photo by L. S. Harrison, NPS 7/85

The **Great Northern Railway Buildings** in Glacier National Park are a National Historic Landmark. The buildings, including Many Glacier Hotel, were constructed by the Great Northern Railway and include five complexes. This site describes the architecture and includes photographs.

The Glacier Park Lodge, located in East Glacier, has the amenities of a first-class resort. Its lobby makes a bold first impression with its enormous Douglas fir pillars. Families can take advantage of the lodge's swimming pool, restaurant, and horse-back tours. It even has two nine-hole golf courses, one of which runs through landscaped gardens.

At Many Glacier Hotel, architects wisely made the windows large. Through the panes of glass, guests can gaze at glaciers, mountain peaks, and the shimmering Swiftcurrent Lake. This hotel, located in Many Glacier Valley, is the largest in the park and is designated as a National Historic Landmark. Guests at the nearby Swiftcurrent Motor Inn can enjoy many of the hotel's services.

The USDA Forest Service has visitor information, and links to sites on plants, mushrooms, tree diseases, and insect identification.

Access this Web site from http://www.myreportlinks.com

The Lake McDonald Lodge Complex dates back to 1913. It was built as a hunting lodge, and animal trophies still decorate the high walls. Famed western artist Charles M. Russell reportedly drew the pictographs on the lobby's enormous stone fireplace. The complex's lodge, cottage, and motor inn rooms are just a short walk from Lake McDonald.

Nearly a century ago, Louis Hill developed nine European-style chalet complexes. Only two of these, Granite Park and Sperry, remain. Because of their remote locations in the mountains, neither is accessible by car. Those willing to stay at Sperry need to hike or ride a horse uphill for 6.5 miles (10.5-kilometers) to get there. Sperry's rooms lack heat, electricity, and running water. Similarly, Granite Park has virtually no amenities. The shortest way to get there is the 4.5-mile (7.2-kilometer) Loop Trail, which features a 2,200-foot (670-meter) change in elevation.

Those on a tight budget have other options. Some visitors stay at the inn and lodge in Apgar Village. Others book reservations at the Rising Sun Motor Inn in St. Mary Valley.

⇨VENTURING OUTSIDE THE PARK

Vacationers can find plenty to do outside of Glacier's borders. Americans are welcome north of the border at Waterton Lakes National Park, which is adjacent to Glacier. Waterton, covering 203 square miles (526 square kilometers), is much smaller than Glacier and attracts fewer visitors. With the exception of glaciers, Waterton boasts natural wonders similar to its sister park to the south. Unlike at Glacier, bison roam the prairies of Waterton. The Prince of Wales Hotel ranks among the park's top attractions. This intricately designed hotel sits high on a bluff overlooking Waterton Lake.

Flathead National Forest, which hugs Glacier's western and southern borders, encompasses 2.3 million acres. About 1 million of these acres are protected wilderness. Flathead offers seventeen hundred miles of roads, twenty-eight hundred miles of hiking trails, and more than thirty small

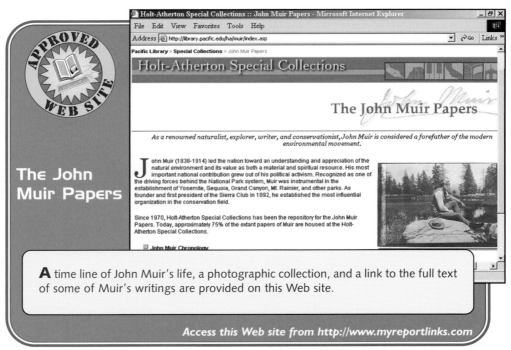

The John Muir Papers

A time line of John Muir's life, a photographic collection, and a link to the full text of some of Muir's writings are provided on this Web site.

Access this Web site from http://www.myreportlinks.com

campgrounds. Fishing and berry picking are other popular activities. Somewhere amid this vast forest, eleven cabins are available for rent. In the winter, two downhill ski resorts attract tourists in the non-wilderness section of the park.

The Flathead Valley, just a few miles west of Glacier, is developing into Montana's playground. Tourists come by the thousands to enjoy golf, rafting, fishing, camping, skiing, and snowmobiling. Adults can enjoy fine dining and art galleries, while children can check out the toy and doll museum and Montana Tom's Chocolate Factory.

An Unforgettable Experience

Because of its remote location, not everyone has the means to travel to Glacier National Park. But if you ever have the opportunity, consider a journey to the "Crown of the Continent." For numberless visitors, their trip has been a life-altering experience.

If you have just a day to spare, make your way through the mountains on Going-to-the-Sun Road. If you have a week, delve deep into this land of lakes and glaciers, sculpted mountains and fascinating animals. John Muir, the great naturalist, recommended an even longer stay. "Give a month at least to this precious reserve," he wrote. "Nevermore will time seem short or long. The time will not be taken from the sum of your life. Instead of shortening it, it will indefinitely lengthen it."[6]

Report Links

The Internet sites described below can be accessed at
http://www.myreportlinks.com

▶**National Park Service: Glacier National Park**
Editor's Choice This National Park Service site provides a very good overview of the park.

▶**Going-to-the-Sun Highway**
Editor's Choice This is an early history of Glacier National Park.

▶**U.S. Geological Survey Photographic Library**
Editor's Choice The U.S. Geological Survey has archival photographs of the park at this site.

▶**National Parks Conservation Association**
Editor's Choice The mission of this nonprofit is to protect and preserve America's national parks.

▶**NASA Earth Observatory: Glacier National Park**
Editor's Choice This site has a satellite image of Glacier.

▶**National Snow and Ice Data Center**
Editor's Choice Find out more about the study of ice.

▶*Blackfoot Lodge Tales*
In this book, Grinnell documents the life and culture of the Blackfoot.

▶**The Crown of the Continent Ecosystem Education Consortium**
This site provides information on mountain ecoregions of the world.

▶**Flathead Lake Biological Station**
Learn more about water when you visit this Web site.

▶**Flathead National Forest**
The goal of this Web site is to give the public reliable information about Flathead.

▶**From the Start, Sun Road Was Designed to Be Spectacular**
Read about the construction of Going-to-the-Sun Road on this site.

▶**George Bird Grinnell**
Learn about the father of American conservation.

▶**Glacier National Park**
For photographs of Glacier National Park, browse this online gallery.

▶**Glacier National Park at a Glance**
This is a comprehensive information guide to Glacier National Park.

▶**Glacier National Park Visitor Information**
Plan your trip to Glacier National Park.

Report Links

▶**Glacier Research**
Glacier monitoring is explained on this site.

▶**Glaciers Disappear in Before & After Photos**
View photos of the glaciers in Glacier National Park.

▶**Glaciers Online**
Learn more about glaciers and view some spectacular photographs.

▶**Great Northern Railway Buildings**
Architecture in Glacier is the subject of this Web site.

▶**Grizzly Bear**
Lots of information on grizzly bears can be found on this site.

▶**History of Glacier National Park**
This National Park Service publication is dedicated to the early history of Glacier.

▶**John Muir Exhibit**
Information on naturalist John Muir, provided by the Sierra Club.

▶**The John Muir Papers**
University of the Pacific provides information on John Muir.

▶***Lewis and Clark***
Visit this PBS site to learn more about Lewis and Clark.

▶**Luxuriant Beargrass**
This site has information on beargrass.

▶***Man in Glacier***
The National Park Service has made available this book about Glacier.

▶**The People . . . Native Americans**
View the Library of Congress's online resources for American Indian culture.

▶**Roosevelt's Tree Army**
This is a brief history of the Civilian Conservation Corps.

▶**Warming Climate Shrinking Glacier Park's Glaciers**
This is an article about the effects of global warming on Glacier.

▶**Warming Clouds National Parks**
This *Chicago Tribune* article discusses global warming and national parks.

algae—Rootless plants that grow in water.

alpine—Referring to high mountain area where it is too cold for trees to grow.

arête—A sharp ridge of rock formed by glaciers on each side.

bane—A curse, or source of ill.

cirque—A bowl-shaped depression eroded out of a mountain by an alpine glacier.

conservationist—A person who advocates the protection of the environment.

Continental Divide—The line that divides the rivers that flow west from the rivers that flow east.

ecology—The study of how organisms interact with one another in their environment.

ecosystem—A community of organisms that interact with one another and the environment in which the organisms live.

environmentalist—A person who strives to protect the environment from pollution or development.

expedition—A journey by a group of people that is organized for a particular purpose.

glacier—An enormous mass of ice that moves slowly downslope due to its own weight.

habitat—The natural home of an animal or a plant.

hanging valley—A river valley or a small canyon that has been cut across by a glacier. It is left at a high elevation above the valley floor.

horn—The peak of a mountain carved by multiple glaciers.

hypothermia—A condition in which one's body temperature becomes dangerously low.

ice age—From thirty-five thousand to twelve thousand years ago, when enormous ice sheets covered much of North America.

marsh—A low-lying wetland with grassy vegetation.

microorganism—An organism that can be seen only through a microscope.

missionary—A person who tries to convert others to his or her religion.

moraine—An accumulation of boulders, rocks, and other matter that is carried and deposited by a glacier.

naturalist—A person who studies and promotes nature.

nonnative—A plant or animal species that originated in a part of the world other than where it currently lives.

plains—A vast area of flat land.

prairie—A broad, treeless, grassy plain.

preservationist—A person who advocates protecting a natural environment with minimal human intervention.

railroad scout—A worker who examines territory and determined the best route for an upcoming railroad.

reservation—Land managed by an American Indian tribe under the U.S. Department of the Interior's Bureau of Indian Affairs.

sediment—Organic material that is transported and deposited by water and wind.

transcontinental railroad—A railway that crosses the continent.

wilderness—Uninhabited land left in its natural condition.

wildflower—A flowering plant that grows on its own, without the help of people.

wildlife—Animals that live in the wilderness.

Chapter 1. Driving to Paradise

1. "Glacier National Park, Montana," *National Geographic*, May 2002, <http://www.nationalgeographic.com/adventure/0205/glacier.html> (January 26, 2007).

2. "Creekland," "Glacier National Park—Our Thoughts," *IgoUgo.com*, October 21, 2006, <http://www.igougo.com/travelcontent/Journal.aspx?JournalID=62003> (January 26, 2007).

3. Susan Bayer Ward, "Going-to-the-Sun Road," *Travel America*, July-August 2003, <http://findarticles.com/p/articles/mi_m0FCQ/is_1_19/ai_104729268> (January 27, 2007).

4. Norma Nickerson, "What the *People* think—Glacier National Park and Vicinity," *Institute for Tourism and Recreation Research*, May 2003, <http://www.itrr.umt.edu/research/NPCAglacier.pdf> (January 28, 2007).

Chapter 2. A Billion Years of History

1. "Glacier National Park, History and Culture," *National Park Service*, n.d., <http://www.nps.gov/glac/historyculture/index.htm> (May 7, 2008).

2. "Shining Mountains Project," British Columbia, n.d., <http://www.env.gov.bc.ca/ecology/bei/shiningmtns.html> (February 4, 2007).

3. Susan Olin, *Insiders' Guide: Glacier National Park* (Guilford, Conn.: The Globe Pequot Press, 2005), p. 25.

4. "Glacier National Park, Historical Overview," *National Park Service*, n.d., <http://www.nps.gov/glac/history/overview.htm> (May 7, 2008).

5. Thomas Schmidt, *Glacier and Waterton Lakes National Parks Road Guide.* Washington: National Geographic Society, 2004, p. 4.

6. Gerald Diettert, "George Bird Grinnell," Missoulian.com, 1999, <http://www.missoulian.com/specials/100montanans/list/045.html> (February 6, 2007).

7. Ibid.

Chapter 3. Glacier's First Century

1. "The National Park System," *National Park Service*, n.d., <http://www.nps.gov/archive/crla/brochures/nps.htm> (February 7, 2007).

2. C. W. Buchholtz, *Man in Glacier,* Glacier Natural History Association, Inc., 1976, <http://www.cr.nps.gov/history/online_books/glac2/chap5.htm> (February 8, 2007).

3. Ibid.

4. C. W. Buchholtz, *Man in Glacier, Glacier Natural History Association*, Inc., 1976, <http://www.cr.nps.gov/history/online_books/glac2/chap5a.htm> (February 8, 2007).

5. Thomas Schmidt, *Glacier and Waterton Lakes National Parks Road Guide, Washington: National Geographic Society*, 2004, p. 4.

6. C. W. Buchholtz, *Man in Glacier, Glacier Natural History Association*, Inc., 1976, <http://www.cr.nps.gov/history/online_books/glac2/chap6.htm> (February 8, 2007).

7. C. W. Buchholtz, *Man in Glacier, Glacier Natural History Association*, Inc., 1976, <http://www.cr.nps.gov/history/online_books/glac2/chap6a.htm> (February 8, 2007).

8. "People, Biodiversity and Ecology," *UNESCO.ORG*, February 3, 2007, <http://www.unesco.org/mab/ecosyst/urban/doc.shtml> (February 9, 2007).

Chapter 4. Full of Life

1. Matthew Brown, "Wolves to be removed from species list," *USA Today*, February 21, 2008, <http://www.usatoday.com/tech/science/2008-02-21-1919579967_x.htm> (August 21, 2008).

2. Gary Turbak, "The bizarre life of the harlequin duck," *National Wildlife,* December 2005–January 2006, <http://www.findarticles.com/p/articles/mi_m1169/is_n1_v35/ai_18911561> (February 14, 2007).

Chapter 5. Threats to the Park

1. Frank Bass and Rita Beamish, "Development Inches Towards National Parks," *San Francisco Chronicle*, June 18, 2006, <http://www.yosemite.org/newsroom/clips2006/june/061806.htm> (February 17, 2007).

2. Norma Nickerson, "What the People think—Glacier National Park and Vicinity," *Institute for Tourism and Recreation Research*, May 2003, <http://209.85.165.104/search?q=cache:jrYsFJIIUoJ:www.itrr.umt.edu/research/NPCAglacier.pdf+%22is+really+unique+terrain.+The+mountains+are+just+gorgeous&hl=en&ct=clnk&cd=1&gl=us&ie=UTF-8> (January 28, 2007).

3. Kirk Johnson, "As Logging Fades, Rich Carve Up Open Land in West," *The New York Times*, October 13, 2007, <http://www.nytimes.com/2007/10/13/us/13timber.html?_r=1&pagewanted=print&oref=slogin> (January 31, 2008).

4. Jonathan Thompson, "The hazy days of summer . . . and winter, spring and fall," *HighCountryNews.org*, June 26, 2006, <http://www.hcn.org/servlets/hcn.Article?article_id=16381> (February 18, 2007).

5. Dave Hadden, "Big Canadian Coal Mine—Big Montana Problem!" *North Fork Preservation Association*, January 22, 2007, <http://www.gravel.org/mt/archives/000237.html> (February 19, 2007).

6. Ibid.

7. "The Case for Restoring Bull Trout to Glacier National Park . . . And a Framework to Do It," *Montana State University*, n.d., <http://64.233.167.104/search?q=cache:-RbKTtVLerAJ:www .montana.edu/mtcfru/GNP%2520Bull%2520Trout%2520Brochure .pdf+%22Fay+Eklund&hl=en&ct=clnk&cd=1&gl=us> (February 19, 2007).

Chapter 6. Exploring Glacier

1. "Glacier National Park and other NPS quotes," *National Park Service*, n.d., <http://www.nps.gov/archive/glac/pdf/ press_quotes.pdf> (February 21, 2007).

2. "Best Easy Day Hikes in Glacier NP Hiking," *Trails .com*, n.d., <http://www.trails.com/activity.asp?area=14815> (February 22, 2007).

3. "Glacier National Park, Montana," *National Geographic*, May 2002, <http://www.nationalgeographic.com/adventure/ 0205/glacier.html> (January 26, 2007).

4. "Glacier National Park Camping Guide," *Glacier.national- park.com*, n.d., <http://www.glacier.national-park.com/camping .htm> (February 23, 2007).

5. Fishing in Glacier National Park, *ParkReservations.com*, n.d., <http://www.parkreservations.com/glacier/fishing.htm> (February 25, 2007).

6. Thomas Schmidt, *Glacier and Waterton Lakes National Parks Road Guide* (Washington: National Geographic Society, 2004), p. 4.

Gildart, Jane, and Bert Gildart. *Glacier National Park and Montana's Flathead Valley.* Kingwood, Tex.: Falcon Publishing, 2007.

Guthrie, C. W. *Glacier National Park: Legends and Lore: Along Going-to-the-Sun Road.* Helena, Mont.: Farcountry Press, 2002.

Hamilton, John. *Glacier National Park.* Edina, Minn.: Abdo Publishers, 2005.

Leftridge, Alan. *Glacier Day Hikes.* Helena, Mont.: Farcountry Press, 2003.

————. *Going to Glacier National Park.* Helena, Mont.: Farcountry Press, 2006.

Lomax, Becky. *Moon Handbooks: Glacier National Park.* Emeryville, Calif.: Avalon Travel Publishing, 2006.

Moravek, Vince. *It Happened in Glacier National Park.* Kingwood, Tex.: Falcon Publishing, 2005.

Olin, Susan. *Glacier National Park.* Guilford, Conn.: The Globe Pequot Press, 2005.

Repanshek, Kurt. *Frommer's National Parks with Kids.* Hoboken, N.J.: Wiley, 2006.

Rockwell, David. *Exploring Glacier National Park.* Kingwood, Tex.: Falcon Publishing, 2002.

Schmidt, Thomas. *Glacier and Waterton Lakes National Parks Road Guide.* Washington: National Geographic Society, 2004.

Walker, Jack. *Roadside Photography Guide to Glacier National Park.* Helena, Mont.: Farcountry Press, 2006.

Yenne, Bill. *Images of America: Glacier National Park.* Mount Pleasant, S.C.: Arcadia Publishing, 2006.